LOVES AND LABOURS

Loves & Labours

AN AUTOBIOGRAPHY
BY PEGGY JAY

in association with Eva Tucker

Weidenfeld and Nicolson
London

First published in 1990 by
George Weidenfeld & Nicolson Limited
91 Clapham High Street, London SW4 7TA

British Library Cataloguing in Publication Data
Jay, Peggy
Loves and labours: an autobiography.
1. England. Social life, 1901 – Biographies
I. Title
942.082'092'4
ISBN 0-297-81025-1

Printed and bound in Great Britain at The Bath Press, Avon

For my grandchildren

Contents

1 CLOUDED CHILDHOOD 1
2 HAMPSTEAD: A LAND OF LOST CONTENT 13
3 THE BOY NEXT DOOR 27
4 FRESH HORIZONS 45
5 THE WAR YEARS 62
6 LABOUR YEARS 77
7 TENSIONS 94
8 THE HEALTH SERVICE AND THE BENCH 109
9 HAMPSTEAD: CONTENTMENT REGAINED 127
INDEX 141

CHAPTER · I

Clouded Childhood

'VERY PLAIN – a great look of Max' was the dry entry in my mother's diary on my birthday, 28 January 1913. There was already a two-year-old son Peter.

My parents, Maxwell Garnett and Margaret Poulton, met in 1909 while playing hockey on the beach in the Isle of Wight. The Garnetts, unlike the Poultons, were also inveterate messers about in boats. My father had shipped across a Canadian canoe when he was still at Cambridge and it was in this that he took Margaret to meet her prospective in-laws. A great storm blew up and she had to lie flat in the bottom of the boat. She arrived hysterical, her evening dress drenched. She almost broke off the engagement.

The Isle of Wight played a central part in my childhood. My happiest memories are of the beloved house on Seagrove Bay belonging to grandfather Garnett, open to the sea in front and to a steep, primrose filled wood at the back. It contrasted sharply with the sunless Manchester house where I spent the first five years of my life, a large proportion of them in a well-scrubbed nursery, complete with green cork floor and ancestral rocking horse. This precious horse had been in the Poulton grandmother's nursery and had the early Victorian pattern, with a curved base swinging up to two small seats. His tail could be removed and as time passed his insides rattled with thimbles, coins and other objects which had been inserted by mischievous small hands. A print of the Dürer hare was later joined by the photograph of Captain Oates with the white ponies on board the *Discovery*, on his way, with Captain Scott, to the Antarctic. A kindly, rather emotional young nanny was my constant attendant. She offered much physical care but little of the magic of play and companionship. I remember the clatter of her feet as she raced up and down the uncarpeted backstairs, carrying a large tin tray to collect our meals from the kitchen. A regular feature of the nursery table were Huntley and Palmer Petit Beurre biscuits and it was through these that I first became aware of the Palmer side of the family, my maternal great-grandparents.

The overall impression of my immediate surroundings was of the Manchester soot which covered the bushes in the garden. Once, at the age of about two, I became aware of a patch of light as I sat on the nursery floor. 'That is the sun' I was told. From time to time, delight burst through the murky monotony of my days in the shape of Aunt Hilda, my father's sister. She had the kindest expression imaginable and had an instinctive love and understanding of small children. Although she had been educated at the North London Collegiate School and Westfield College, Hilda had fallen into the role, so widespread in Victorian and Edwardian times, of the unmarried daughter living at home. She was expected to abandon her Sunday Bible class in order to cut sandwiches for her mother's 'At Home' day. Hilda was a deeply spiritual person whose Christian convictions were fulfilled in Anglo-Catholicism. Though her visits were infrequent, the whole world lit up for me when she came. We would ride on a tram to buy a doll's pram, and when we went to a children's service in the church across the road I would light a candle happily forgetting nanny's protests about the risk in doing so. She took me to a nursery school run by a friend in a poor district of Manchester which, to an only child like me, seemed an enchanted world. When she left, I fell back into the humdrum routine of walks in Victoria Park, endless milk puddings, conversations with the dust-covered hens who lived in the old stables and visits downstairs to my parents.

Golden-haired, tall and stately, my mother fitted perfectly into the drawing room she had created. Her flowing garments, in clear William Morris colours and designs, blended with the peacock fireplace and Liberty prints on the sofas. Her tastes were in advance of her times – no blinds, lace curtains or general clutter for her. But she had little time for the whims and wishes of a young child. For her the training of children fell into the same category as the training of dogs. Occasionally, when I came downstairs after tea, a very beautiful wax doll was brought out from where it lay hidden in layers of tissue paper. But so many were the warnings to take great care that it was difficult to enjoy playing with it.

At weekends my father was there, too, relaxed in shorts and sweater, sporting his pink Leander scarf. Then there were the fun and games – the times alone with my mother are not memorable for either. He was a kind father, talking me patiently through tearful crises when my mother had abandoned me in disgust. I remember, on one occasion, screaming on the floor in protest at the scratchy combinations I was made to wear. He picked me up, looked at me with his benevolent, very blue eyes and soothed me through what seemed an unbearable situation. On the Isle of Wight holidays he would put me gently into his Canadian canoe and we would paddle peacefully to the next village. There I would proudly follow his tall, seabooted figure up the main street to the boatbuilders where I enjoyed the smell of rope and tar while he bought his tackle.

Life at home was mostly harmonious, for my parents' marriage was based on deep mutual respect. My mother gave my father her wholehearted support in his idealistic strivings, both in his educational work in Manchester and later, in his work for the League of Nations Union. Her own preferences were for animals and flowers and my father loved to indulge her, though it might possibly have been better for her had he idolized her a little less.

From 1914 onwards, however, a number of tragedies overshadowed their life together. First came the death of my three-year-old brother Peter. He died the day after an operation for the removal of a brain tumour, since at that date the techniques of blood transfusion were unknown. The loss of this first-born, fair-haired, blue-eyed little boy, the eldest grandchild on both sides of the family, was a crushing blow. My mother once said that after Peter's death she never felt completely happy again. Although I was only twelve months old at the time, there is no doubt that my brother's death had a profound effect on my own early childhood. I was constantly aware of my parents' grief. I remember an occasion in the Manchester drawing room when my father left abruptly. My mother explained to me that he had gone upstairs to weep for his lost son. Clearly, no one actually dared to utter the question: why did God take the boy and leave the girl? But I sensed that this was what they felt. I look here, to these very early years, for the origins of my own restless, striving spirit, always longing to be recognized and approved of, and above all, to *achieve*.

For a considerable time, my mother failed to have the further children both parents wanted. She had a succession of miscarriages, initially caused by the shock and grief over her son's death. I remember her in bed, either at home, or away for months, being nursed at her parents' home in Oxford. The Poulton grandparents lived all their married lives in a large, typical North Oxford house at the Parks end of the Banbury Road. Grandmother Emily Poulton's family were Quakers, the Palmers of Reading. In the eighteenth century they had married into another Quaker family, the Clarks, who made shoes at Street in Somerset. Since industrial enterprises like steel, which led to the manufacture of armaments were forbidden to Quakers, George Palmer with his partner Thomas Huntley, set up the famous biscuit firm of Huntley and Palmer in Reading in 1841. George Palmer later became Liberal MP for Reading. One of my grandmother's sisters, Alice Palmer, married Augustus Waller FRS, who was one of Augustus Waller's medical students. Following his engagement to her, he found the blackboard in his lecture room bearing the message 'Waller takes the biscuit!' With characteristic wit, Waller added '... and the tin' – no less than £1 million! Alice's two sisters were similarly endowed.

George Palmer's son George William, followed in his footsteps and was made Privy Councillor in 1906, a rare distinction for a backbench MP. The honour was conferred in recognition of his distinguished services to Reading in the improvement of housing and sanitation and the creation of open spaces. My grandmother was George William's sister. When she married Edward Poulton, a young Oxford don, her father gave her a pearl necklace which was intended to compensate her for having to move to Oxford 'where the conversation would be so bad'. My grandparents' Oxford house had been built by an ex-chef from New College and was called Wykeham House; it had a statue and a coat of arms of William of Wykeham. John Ruskin is said to have commended the preservation of this house as representing a perfect example of the awfulness of Gothic revival. Queen Victoria's youngest son, Prince Leopold, lived there in the 1850s as an undergraduate. He was deeply in love with the young daughter of the Dean of Christ Church, none other than Lewis Carroll's Alice.

I felt utterly useless and bewildered on those visits to my mother's bedside and escaped as soon as I could to go and suck my thumb and talk to Pepper, the grey parrot with the scarlet tail, in the hall. A few years later, when I was away at Malvern Girls' College I was cheered to receive a letter from this parrot headed 'The Hall, Near Window Seat'. It said 'I hear that you are very fond of dogs, horses, guinea pigs and such creatures.

I want to remind you that in some respects *we* are a superior order of beings. We have a higher temperature and feathers are very superior to hair for beauty and as a covering. Also we can fly and our bodies are lighter and stronger for their weight and size. So please extend your love and sympathy to us. I wish you many happy returns of the day and have specially pulled out this feather today as a birthday present.' By a strange coincidence, Pepper's handwriting was exactly like my zoologist grandfather Poulton's.

My mother poured out her anxieties in letters to my father. They sometimes wrote to each other two or three times a day. 'The wretched doctor was heartbreakingly vague – I don't feel at all optimistic'. Her own father urged her not to dress, or dress her hair, until after the eighteenth week of pregnancy. Sometimes she rallied her spirits with Prime Minister Asquith's famous words 'Wait and see'.

My father volunteered for the Armed Forces at the outbreak of war in 1914. He had a First in Mathematics from Trinity College, Cambridge and became a wrangler. After Cambridge, he worked in the Ministry of Education, but, with his pioneering spirit, he felt restless in the Civil Service world. In 1912 he became Principal of what was then the Manchester College of Technology. He was rejected for service in the Forces because he had bad varicose veins in his legs, inoperable in those days. The authorities considered that the rigours of army life would be too much for him. He got over his disappointment by heaving coal when it was delivered and digging a cutting through a bank in the garden which, he told me, was what the soldiers in France were doing.

In May 1915 came the news that my mother's brother, Ronald, had been killed in Flanders by a stray bullet. Ronald was a committed, enthusiastic social reformer. He was convinced that the way forward for the country was by progress towards partnership between employers and employed. At first he was reluctant to accept the great fortune (and responsibilities) which the inheritance of the Palmer biscuit money placed upon him. Even though he only had the inheritance for two years, he concentrated on sharing it and, in his will, the Workers' Educational Association was one of the organizations he especially remembered.

His work in industrial Manchester and Reading, in the Boys' Clubs, was his apprenticeship for what he hoped would be the opportunity to fulfil his ideals on a wider stage. Dr William Temple, his close friend from Rugby and Balliol days, later Archbishop of Canterbury, wrote about him in 1909, referring to Plato's concept of the absolute, 'the absolute had literally (in Ronald) appeared before him. Everything else seemed subordinate to this; his skill in games, his self-sacrifice for the boys in the clubs he helped to manage, his hopes of reform in the industrial world, based on the growth of understanding and sympathy between employers and employed, all seemed part of that extraordinary lovableness – its modes of manifestation and action.' Ronald was an International rugby player and captain of the 1914 England team. He had the charisma of the great athlete, though he was, of course, much more than that. William Temple wrote of his last meeting with Ronald in March 1915, only two months before he was killed: 'Ronald was very sad for he had lately lost several close friends. He said "I don't want to be killed yet, there is such a lot I wanted to do, try, anyhow." I asked if he felt he would be killed. "Oh yes" he said "sure of it." I said nothing, and again there was a long silence. Then he suddenly said "Of course, it's all right, but it's not what one would have chosen."'

My mother and their elder brother, Edward Poulton, went to visit Ronald in quarters with his battalion in Swindon. 'It was a pathetic little visit, walking in the streaming rain. After tea in the mess we had a long talk in the refreshment room at the railway station. Next day, while walking to Bucklebury on the beautiful Sunday evening, and during the service in the lovely little old church, the tragedy of the whole thing overwhelmed me with terrible force; I seemed to see the end then,' she wrote. Theirs was a particularly close brother-sister relationship. His last letter written to his 'Darling Mags' was dated the day he was killed. I recently met someone who had been cook in my parents' first home. She described the joyous and noisy reunions when Ronald visited. 'We in the kitchen thought the ceiling would fall down', as brother and sister romped in the sitting room upstairs.

Ronald was shot through the heart, probably by a sniper, on 5 May 1915. His company wept as he was buried at dawn in the little Belgian wood at Ploegsteert. The memorial service in Rugby School Chapel was held jointly for him and Rupert Brooke. Fifty years later, I would sometimes meet elderly men who, on hearing I was Ronald's niece, were visibly upset.

In the following year, on 24 September 1916, my father's younger brother, Stuart Garnett, was killed in experimental flying for the Royal Flying Corps on Salisbury Plain. He was a scholar at St Paul's school and Trinity College, Cambridge, and gained a First in the Mechanical Science Tripos in 1903. He wrote a book on turbines and after a short time as master at Eton, he was called to the Bar. His book *Children and the Law* was for many years regarded as a blueprint in dealing with youngsters and foreshadowed by many years the setting up of juvenile courts. By this time, Stuart was living in Toynbee Hall from which he moved to a small council flat. He ran a club for men and boys in the evenings which gave rise to the Ratcliffe Sea Scouts. He restored an old fourteen foot sailing dinghy which he and his sea scouts sailed in the English Channel and the North Sea. This boat is still in family use after nearly eighty years. He was awarded the Royal Cruising Cup on three occasions for sailing Enterprises in the Orkneys and Shetlands.

At the outbreak of war, Stuart joined the RNVR and went to sea, in command of an armed yacht called the *Zareefah*. His crew was a combination of Cambridge friends and his Sea Scouts. He worked on minesweeping and later this vessel became the flagship of the Admiral in command of Channel minesweeping. In 1915 he joined the Royal Flying Corps and when, in 1916, he was transferred to do experimental work on Salisbury Plain, he crashed to his death during a trial flight.

In 1917, my father's youngest brother, Kenneth Garnett, died from wounds received the previous year in the Battle of the Somme. I think it was his death that my grandparents and aunt found the hardest to bear. He was a sunny, cheerful character. A newspaper picture shows him looking splendid in his Leander rowing outfit, swinging down to the river at Henley in 1914. He was a blond giant of six feet four inches, the tallest man ever to row in the Cambridge Boat. He had brotherly friendships with the schoolgirl sisters of his friends, but in a letter to an infant godson, to be read when he was older, he urged extreme caution in relations with young women. 'Never go near a skirt', he wrote, revealing his non-conformist background. This also showed itself in my father of whom it was said that when he married he had never read a novel, been to the theatre or kissed a girl.

Of course, I was very young when all this happened but I remember Kenneth in khaki, tall and fair, standing smiling up at me on the stairs in my Garnett grandparents' Hampstead home 'The Chestnuts' and me, aged four, gazing down at him. I have no recollection of Stuart, but I remember his young blonde widow, Sybil, lying on a sofa in this same house awaiting the birth of his posthumous son.

During these years my mother also lost both her sisters. The eldest, another Hilda and also my godmother, died of what was then called Graves Disease (goitre) in 1917. She was still in her twenties. I remember visiting her bedside and being fascinated by the bag of ice easing her throat and also by her small dog. My mother was very close to this sister and her death caused her enormous grief. Indeed, my mother had hoped to have a baby specifically to give to this childless sister – Hilda was married to a doctor – and this some seventy years before the controversies of surrogate motherhood.

The youngest sister, Janet, was killed in 1919 when her cycle mudguard jammed in the wheel and she was thrown over the handlebars. Her husband, Sir Charles Symonds, had survived four years of war in France. She had once said to her father about him 'if only all the family didn't like him so much, I should find it much easier to accept his proposal of marriage'. I remember walking with her and her two infant sons in a country lane. She was pushing the pram with her new baby, Richard, while his two-year-old brother, Ronald, screamed, no doubt with frenzied jealousy. Janet felt that this 'naughtiness' should be followed up by firm action and he found himself dumped in the hedgerow.

The deep sadness caused by all these deaths was in some measure mitigated when in 1917, to my parents' great joy, another girl was born. I was nearly five years old. My sister Hilda Rebecca Pauline arrived in August 1917, three weeks after the death of my mother's elder sister, Hilda. I had no idea there was to be a new baby and so when I was taken into my mother's bedroom to see a baby on the nurse's lap, my reaction was one of shock rather than pleasure. During the next ten years the arrival of another sister and three brothers confused my emotions, since no one ever prepared me for these events. At one level, I was glad, even proud; on another level, my jealousy was inflamed by my parents' obvious pride and joy in their growing family. Now, in my middle seventies, I can confess to echoes of this same jealousy when I am with my children and grandchildren. To be alone with my grandchildren is total pleasure, to be with them in their parents' company is to relive the insecurities and jealousies of the small child who felt pushed out by her younger sisters and brothers.

In 1918 my father took me to the Armistice celebrations in

central Manchester. Vast crowds of people in dark clothes waved flags hysterically and, surrounded by their dancing feet, I wondered why they wept as they danced. After Armistice, the shreds of family life were gathered together and the adults made valiant efforts to recreate a semblance of past happiness. Manchester was a seedbed of intellectuals, social reformers, writers and thinkers, and though social life in my parents' circle was low key, there were dinner parties to which friends like Ernest and Shena Simon (later Lord and Lady Simon of Wythenshawe) were invited, and Mary Stocks, later Baroness Stocks, as well as Eva Hubback, an old Manchester friend of my mother's whose husband had been killed in 1917. There were, too, social occasions at the Technical College, where my father was Principal. Once, at the age of four, I had to present a bouquet to the vast and bejewelled Shah of Persia.

My father was battling with the authorities in Manchester to raise the educational status of the Technical College and to have it incorporated in the University of Manchester (UMIST today). He lost this battle and when, in 1919, the education committee decided to limit the number of degree students and to admit some senior technical schoolboys as full-time students, my father resigned.

I spent the long summer of 1919 learning to read and to swim with my Garnett grandparents and aunt in 'the house on the beach' at Horestone Point, in the Isle of Wight. My father's father, Dr William Garnett, came from a Huguenot family called Orange who were said to have arrived in an open boat at Portsmouth harbour after the Revocation of the Edict of Nantes. He was born at Portsea in 1850, the son of an auctioneer. The family moved to London and he won a scholarship to the City of London School, where the future Prime Minister H.H. Asquith was also a pupil. In their final year at the school, Asquith was head of the classical sixth and my grandfather head of the mathematical sixth. Years later, when he was looking for a holiday house for his family, he took the small ferry from Southsea to Seaview Pier (which was destroyed in a storm in the late 1950s) on the Isle of Wight and found what he was looking for – in Seagrove Bay. He bought the last of a group of houses being erected by a local builder, though he was warned that the unstable soil would make it disappear into the sea in forty years time. 'That's as long as I shall need it' he said. (In fact, the house collapsed in 1943, following vibrations from naval gunfire and the dropping of sea mines which caused severe tremors.)

In pre-1914 days, the two large families, approaching in groups from their respective villages, would see each other every Sunday across the cornfield on their way to attend the Service – the Poultons wending their way from St Helens along the footpath through the cornfields, while the Garnetts approached from Seaview, the footpaths converging at the church.

In June 1919 my brother Michael Ronald Kenneth, named after the dead uncles, was born. He arrived on the Isle of Wight carried by a nanny in a procession of parents and luggage. I galloped towards them, pretending to be a pony. At the end of the summer we went back to Manchester, but soon after this my father heard that the infant League of Nations Union under its President Lord Cecil and its Chairman Professor Gilbert Murray were looking for a General Secretary. He rushed up to London and was offered the appointment. My mother wept with relief at the news. And so, with our move to Hampstead, where my parents had lived when they were first married, the 1920s began on a note of new hope.

CHAPTER · 2

Hampstead: A Land of Lost Content

EVEN IN 1920, Hampstead and the Heath were for me 'a land of lost content' and the wartime visits to The Chestnuts, my Garnett grandparents' house in Branch Hill overlooking Constable's pond, were full of happiness. I remembered toy yachts flying before the wind on the Whitestone Pond, the tall flagstaff and the anti-aircraft gun which flashed blue fountains of light into the night; walks to feed the stately deer in Golders Hill Park, and visits to the white fire-station horses which lived under the clock tower, opposite the Hampstead tube.

But now Hampstead was home. We lived in an enormous redbrick house, one of four, built in the garden of the beautiful eighteenth-century Foley House. The Garnett grandparents had lived at Number 4 Foley Avenue in the 1890s, we were at Number 1, which was later known as 21 Well Walk. At that time, it was not considered an unreasonable sized home for a youngish professional man and his growing family. Its main feature was the central hall with shining varnished pitch-pine (much disliked by my mother, and later stripped to a gentle pale bloom); ornate carved wooden columns, double doors (which could be removed for parties) and a parquet floor. A wide, stone spiral staircase led down to the dining room, kitchen and front door.

One of our neighbours in Foley Avenue was J.B. Priestley and his young family. Priestley, resplendent in white flannels, could be heard shouting 'Anyone for tennis'? from the Gainsborough Gardens court behind Foley Avenue, but it was the constant yelling of his infants from the neighbouring garden which finally drove my mother to seize her pen and write to the *New Statesman*. Those were the days of Truby King: no infant could be fed until the clock struck the appointed hour. My mother argued, to my intense embarrassment as a young schoolgirl, that since dogs and cats fed their young on demand, there was no reason why humans should not do likewise. This letter was typical of my parents' independence of spirit. Though they fell into the conventional pattern of their day in may ways, where things they felt strongly about were concerned, they had no hesitation in breaking the mould – much to the consternation of friends and neighbours.

The Jays were our immediate neighbours at the Well Road end of our garden. The eldest son was at Dartmouth Naval College; the second, Douglas, at Winchester; and the two daughters at Frognal School. The comings and goings of these older children fascinated me. I had an enchanting turret bedroom in the new house with four windows looking out over London to St Paul's and, on clear days, to the Surrey hills. But up there, I did not really feel part of the expanding family life. When the closed door of my parents' bedroom opened from time to time and a nurse rustled out in her starched apron with a white bundle in her arms, I was sent to picnic with aunts Hilda and Dorothy in the fields off the Finchley Road where the Express Dairy cows enjoyed their days.

The first Hampstead baby was born in 1921 and he was named John William Poulton Maxwell. His second name, William, was in honour of Uncle Ronald's great friend, Archbishop Temple. I associated John's birth with the noise and clatter of a Hampstead August Bank Holiday Monday. We returned from the quiet hayfield off the Finchley Road into the milling crowds streaming up to the Heath, to find a large, blond baby boy at home. I was delighted with him and though at the age of nine I could hardly foresee the lifelong love and support which John was to give me, the rapport with him was immediate.

So the small children lived their separate lives with nannies, prams, high chairs and birthday parties. Sometimes I felt left out and suffered pangs of resentment that my parents should be so preoccupied with people and things that had nothing to do with me. So, overcome by acute feelings of jealousy, I would tease my younger brothers and sisters, especially, for instance, when the after-tea games in the drawing room were too infantile for me to enjoy. Sometimes I persecuted the nannies, choosing to cast them in the role of 'oppressors' of the underdogs, i.e. the little ones. Nor was I part of my parents' lives. My mother liked to arrange tulips on the grand piano, where, behind her, was a large oil painting of herself, the blue flowing draperies setting off her golden hair, fair skin and firm jaw. Her housekeeping was not burdensome. Each morning, after she had interviewed the cook, she would telephone for deliveries. At the end of the week she went to local shops to 'pay the books', a serious and immovable duty of the housewives of the day. Every Monday a lady came from a cottage in Flask Walk to do the family washing; she boiled it in a large zinc bath and mangled it with wooden rollers. The rule of the house demanded that the washing line must be removed by the afternoon and must, of course, never be seen at weekends.

My mother was a keen gardener, so keen, in fact, that when General Election day came she said she was too busy in the garden to go and vote – and this in spite of the 'Votes for Women' carved plaque up in her kitchen!

My father was deeply involved with the League of Nations Union. He frequently arrived home late and by the time we heard his key in the door and his walking-stick rattling in the stand we were often very hungry. I was allowed down to dinner from the age of ten. On the one hand, this meant I had to change out of my school uniform; on the other, it was something of a privilege and meant I could enjoy my parents' company without the distraction of the younger children. I was aware that great issues were at stake as my father spoke of Manchuria and later of Abyssinia. Quite often he took me with him to his office in Grosvenor Crescent, marching across Hyde Park Corner, holding out his walking-stick to delay the traffic. My feelings of loyalty towards my father were intense, and once, when I was about ten, I insisted on walking home because I could not bear to hear the driver of the car belittling the work of the League of Nations.

I also remember feeling mystified by requests to be absolutely quiet when my parents were closeted behind closed doors in the library. They were, in fact, deep in discussion over family finances which involved the mysterious process of 'selling out capital'. All this left me with the quite erroneous impression that whatever happened there would always be a financial safety net. How false and disastrous this assumption proved to be!

My own life was centred on the rabbits I kept in an old cycle shed at the end of the garden. The pains and joys of rabbit family life were a constant concern and I was immensely upset to discover that a father rabbit would eat his young if he was left with the mother.

The Heath seemed an extension of our garden as we wandered across East Heath Road in a procession of prams, cycles and dogs. Dogs played a significant part in my childhood. My mother had always been very fond of them and now the Irish terrier Pompey, of Manchester days, had been succeeded by a Bedlington terrier called Pax. My sister, Pauline, remembers meeting our mother walking this dog on the Heath when the three young children were out with their nanny. My mother did not reciprocate their enthusiasm at the encounter, she preferred the company of the dogs to that of her three youngest children. The nanny of those days was a remarkable Miss Woods, who came to us from the Victor Gollancz family. I did not have much to do with her, but was aware of the harmony her influence exercised over the children.

On Sundays we regularly attended either Hampstead Parish Church, Christchurch, or the Congregational Church, at the corner of Lyndhurst Road, which we knew as Dr Horton's. My father, who read his Greek Testament every day of his life, dominated Sunday lunchtime discussions of the sermon we had just heard and we children were encouraged to take part. I remember reference to the school at Bembridge on the Isle of Wight having two pulpits which, my father explained, enabled the boys to hear both sides of every question!

In 1922 I was sent to Frognal School, In our large velour hats, with red and green bands, we proudly crossed the High Street watching carefully for the occasional vehicle. On Sports Day on the Heath Extension I proudly wore a miniature medal with its red and green ribbon gained for running, acutely anxious that my small brothers and sisters and attendant dogs should not misbehave and draw unwanted attention from my seniors. Then, in 1923, came a day when, weeping profusely, I told my parents I wanted to go to boarding school. I was increasingly at odds with family life and was considered difficult to manage. Both my mother and I had hot tempers on a short fuse. Her idea of child management was to tell me what to do and not to think about myself. There was constant conflict over table manners, tidiness and clothes. I also secretly felt that perhaps I was cleverer than my mother. She had unconventional tastes in architecture and interior decoration and liked plants and animals. But quick verbal repartee was beyond her and in numerous tempestuous scenes I was accused of rudeness and reduced to tears.

I loathed my four terms at Malvern Girls' College, chosen because my great-aunt Lily Poulton had started it, before the

Great War, in her front room. I had arrived with a vast trunk of expensive school uniform, including a white serge coat and a skirt for going to church on Sundays. The Draconian discipline, I felt, represented the worst aspect of a boys' public school. I remember a scene of Dickensian terror as a large and choleric house mistress raved at me for not extending my little finger as I drank from the cup. The high point of our regulated school days were expeditions up the Malvern Hills. In spite of those 'blue remembered hills' of Housman's poems, I felt ill with homesickness. My mother's handwriting on an envelope made me tremble with excitement, though the contents of the envelope did not always live up to expectations. One letter began 'It is our wedding day today, just fancy, thirteen years ago we were married and if Peter had lived, he would have been twelve years old!' No amount of news about fluffy kittens which followed could make up for the pain this kind of reminder caused me.

The letters I had from my Garnett grandmother also failed to cheer a homesick little girl. 'We want each year to leave some fault behind, don't we'? she wrote for my eleventh birthday. 'Think darling which sin you are determined shall not enter into this fresh year and so make stepping stones to heaven. There is a ladder reaching from earth to heaven and the angels of God go up and down all the time to help all those who are beginning to climb ... Put out your hand, it will be held by some angel of help and go up one step. The next will be easier. The first is pretty hard but you are a climber, aren't you? Don't slip back ...' The extent of my wretchedness is reflected in a letter to my father. 'My darling, darling Daddy, I love you so very very much, very very, *very* much indeed. I was so sad when I heard it was your birthday cause I didn't give you *any* birthday present but perhaps it's rather like a little tiny sort of birthday present because I'm trying very hard with my letters, really I am daddy darling.' The letter continues describing a visit to tea with Aunt Lily Poulton as 'such fun', a white lie which I probably felt deserved a little reward for the letter ends 'Do you think daddy darling you could send me a little tiny bit more sweeties'? I certainly missed my Hampstead home enormously and there is no doubt that I was 'easier to manage' when I left Malvern and got back home for good. So my experience of boarding school proved to be an unhappy one. But then, I was an unhappy, insecure child. Many years later I saw my grandchildren settle readily and happily into boarding school life, for their parents had spent a great deal of time with them in early childhood. It was Dr John Bowlby who established in the 1940s that the more dependent a child is allowed to be in its earliest days, the more independent it becomes later.

In September 1924, just before I was twelve years old, I entered St Paul's Girls' School. It was the best thing that had happened to me. This great girls' school, a splendid building with its own music wing, swimming bath and gymnasium, had been opened in 1904 by King Edward VII who expressed the hope that it would offer opportunities *almost* as good as those the boys had in the St Paul's of ancient foundation in Hammersmith. At my entrance exam, I was interviewed by the High Mistress, Miss Gray. Her white hair was piled high and smooth on her head and dressed in her full, long, black academic gown, she was an awe-inspiring figure. She asked me to read the passage in Matthew Arnold's *Scholar Gypsy* about the 'Dons on the Dais'. Thanks to visits to my Poulton grandfather's Oxford college, I knew what a dais was.

Miss Gray had had the music wing, with its carefully designed music hall and practice rooms above, built in honour of Gustav Holst, who taught music at the school. I can still see his gold-rimmed glasses flashing as he lost himself conducting the school orchestra, the music often his own. The other members of the staff at St Paul's were all unmarried, high-minded, hard-working, very intelligent women. They expected and got, good quality work from us. Our form mistress Miss Wigg wrote a touching letter when I left saying how greatly she would miss our group; Miss Watt, who taught history, and Miss Patrick, who taught geography, remained objects of affection and gratitude for many years.

We were quite unselfconscious as girls in a boys' world. We wore black bowler hats, strapped on cricket pads and declined Latin verbs. We regarded ourselves as *boys* in a boys' world and we certainly did not feel inferior to them. My father and his two brothers had been scholars at St Paul's and proudly wore the silver fish, the scholar's insignia, on their watch chains. So, in a sense, I was going to the old school and my father felt proud of me. He caused me some embarrassment, though, when he taught me to play lacrosse, for the fending-off operation used by men was regarded as 'rough' in the girls' game and I was sometimes sent off the field. I have to confess that the games we played were my greatest pleasure at school. I was something of a swimmer and a gymnast and also played lacrosse for the school. When I was awarded the coveted broad white girdle I took it to my father, who was recovering from an operation in a nursing home, and he hung it proudly near his bed.

I was more conscious of my seniors than my juniors at school. Celia Johnson was still there when I arrived and it was a special pleasure when, sixty years later, I was asked to become involved in the building of the Celia Johnson Memorial Theatre at the school. My immediate seniors included Nicolette Binyon (whose father, Laurence, came to speak to us on poetry) and Anne Scott-James, who later gained a first in Honour Mods at Somerville and left Oxford to become knitting editor of *Vogue*. Both these girls were scholars, as was my contemporary, Diana Hubback. Before I actually started at St Paul's, my mother had asked her old Manchester friend, Eva Hubback, to tea with Diana, whom I had not yet met. I refused to be present at this tea party because Diana was going to the school as a scholar! She and Shiela Grant Duff were in the fast-moving top stream and I was in the second stream. But after my father had had an interview with the High Mistress, I too found myself in the top stream. Shiela and Diana were 'best friends', drawn to each other, no doubt, because both had lost their fathers during the Great War. I was fascinated by Shiela from the moment I first saw her. She looked like a young Viking queen, her thick corn-coloured hair blown back, wearing a butcher blue shirt even though our uniform demanded round-necked white blouses with our navy serge tunics. So one day, while I was sitting on Willesden junction platform with Diana, waiting for the train to take us home, wafts of sour milk from the milk churns assailing our nostrils, I plucked up courage and asked her if she would let Shiela be *my* best friend. Diana more or less handed me Shiela on a plate as Maire Lynd had become *her* best friend.

The St Paul's of the 1920s did not touch on the disturbing problem of the opposite sex and, indeed, apart from the occasional remote father in a friend's house, I seldom met any men or boys. So, we were thrown back on each other in our emotional lives. I remember illicitly sitting on the floor in one of the practice rooms with Shiela, reading a shared copy of Rosamond Lehmann's *Dusty Answer*. We were drawn irresistibly to this novel, aware of matters beyond our understanding. Shiela had had Robert Graves's *Goodbye to All That* removed from her at home.

I have kept the immensely long letters which Shiela and I sent to each other, when we were apart even for a weekend, and am amazed that we had time to read, let alone write, them. My mother always said I bullied Shiela. 'If Peggy wanted to go on the top of a bus and you wanted to go inside, you would go on top' she once said to Shiela. But this was not the whole truth, for in may ways, I needed her more than she needed me. Shiela's mother saw this.

Then there were my companions on the long journey to school: Sighle and Maire, the daughters of the poet Robert Lynd. Anna Jane and Justin Blanco White were another pair of sisters with whom I travelled. Their mother, Amber Reeves, had been the heroine of H.G.Wells's novel *Ann Veronica*. Indeed, Anna Jane was Wells's daughter, a fact both amazing and incomprehensible to me, but I watched and listened to them with fascination as we did our homework on the Broad Street line train, often with a whole carriage to ourselves. The long climb up East Heath Road on the way home was sometimes enlivened by the unwinding of a treasured golf ball on a long elastic string. When I got back home to the house in Well Walk, either cold and hungry or hot and hungry, there would be a splendid tea tray complete with a kipper waiting for me.

In my later school days I had my hair cut off and styled into an Eton crop and thought I cut a dash in a pair of men's grey flannels. Round about this time the John Colet Society at school invited Harold Laski to talk to us about Communism and he quoted Macaulay's dictum 'to reform if you would preserve is the watchword of great events'. I worried my mother by my refusal to concern myself with domestic matters. She always said I would sooner read the newspaper in which the fish was wrapped than unwrap the fish. In the end, she wrote to St Paul's asking if we could have some 'domestic science' in the curriculum. She was firmly told that shortage of time, staff and materials made such an innovation impossible.

I was working on an essay about T.H.Huxley whom my Poulton grandfather had known. 'I will tell you how the great man died', he said in a letter to me in May 1925. 'There was a tremendously cold winter in the early months of 1895 ... This intense cold weakened Huxley and then he got influenza, and then he had bronchitis and other lung trouble. This went on for four months and then he threw it off, but his heart was weakened by it, and then the kidney trouble began. His brain was so strong that when the doctors said he had the kidney illness, he said they must be wrong, because if it was what they said, he ought to be unconscious. The doctors were astonished. Then his heart failed and he died on 29 June 1895. He was buried at Finchley, rather near Hampstead, I think'. Such graphic links with the great man of the fairly recent past had an inspiring effect on me.

In 1925 my youngest sister, Priscilla Janet Cecil, was born in the Well Walk house (Cecil after my father's colleague Lord Robert Cecil). I remember lurking in the hall, aged twelve, listening to frantic telephone conversations. Eventually a female figure (my mother believed in having a woman doctor) ascended the stairs, in full evening dress, complete with jet hangings and medical bag in hand. She was a consultant and had come straight from an evening engagement to help a tiny five-pound sister into the world and sort out the *placenta praevia*. The first indication I had had that another baby was imminent was the setting up of the cradle, with its white muslin frill, topped by dark and pale blue satin ribbon to remind us of our parents' loyalties to both the ancient universities.

We spent holidays in the 1920s with the two sets of grandparents in the Isle of Wight. In April and August, and early September, the family (by 1927 there were five children) stayed either at St Helen's cottage with my mother's parents, the Poultons, or at Horestone Point, the house on the beach near Seaview which belonged to my father's parents, the Garnetts. The tensions of three generations under one roof were increasingly felt. At St Helen's the grandparents insisted on total silence for two hours in the afternoon, while they rested. On one disastrous occasion, my father dropped a shoe in the bedroom, above the study, during this sacred time. He was frightened to disturb my grandfather even more and carefully removed the second shoe. At tea, he was informed that further rest had proved impossible, as my grandfather had been on the alert, waiting for the second shoe to drop.

We also had problems with the lack of space. In August 1927 my mother wrote to my father 'Mother writes that she will have no room for you and Peggy. I must try and get a room in the village for you and we must stick it out this summer – being apart.' My Poulton grandparents were still clearly mourning the loss of three of their children in the previous decade. When grandfather Poulton bought St Helen's Common, the land opposite his house, he gave it to the National Trust in memory of these three children who had died in their twenties.

My uncle Edward remained – Dr E. P. Poulton of Guy's Hospital – who spent the summer in the converted stables, known as the Annexe, with his wife and children. The only other surviving Poulton child was my mother. Quite apart from the enforced rest period, life at St Helen's cottage had a ceremonial quality which was hardly child-oriented. The arrival of a small donkey cart heralded the erection on the beach of a large two-compartment tent. Here grandmother Poulton, accompanied by her maid, would change for her daily swim. My cousin Teddy Poulton once told me that he so dreaded the St Helen's Cottage holidays that when the taxi arrived to take them he would run and hide in the vegetable garden.

In 1926 my mother received a legacy from her uncle, Alfred Palmer, (of Huntley and Palmer biscuit fame). With it she was able to buy Horestone Point and the surrounding land, a beautiful corner of the Isle of Wight. Priory Bay was, and still is, unspoilt by building or, indeed, by people. In summer, the white smooth sands, and the azure sea dotted with its flying sails, are reminiscent of the Caribbean. My mother's first thought was to find an architect who would build a family holiday-house worthy of this magical site. She found Oliver Hill. He had already built a house in Bembridge for Sir John Betjeman's parents-in-law, about which Betjeman wrote a satirical poem. Oliver Hill proved the answer to all my mother hoped for. She wrote to my father 'I had the most satisfactory and jolly interview with Oliver Hill, I have supreme confidence in his taste, which is such a comfort.'

On the highest point of the land, Oliver Hill designed a white house with a steep-pitched green tiled roof. The house had a great feeling of openness to the view, the sea and the sun. A descending curved wall around the house created the impression of a ship, best seen from the coast, in full sail. The balcony outside my parents' bedroom was a replica of Nelson's quarter deck in the *Victory*.

My mother came down on day trips from London and as she walked up the long leafy lane towards the house she could hear, across the fields, the tap-tap of carpenters at work. As she neared the house, the delicious smell of fresh wood shavings greeted her nostrils. My parents had tremendous respect for all forms of skilled craftsmanship. They had the staircase window inscribed not only with their names and the names of their children, but also with the names of all the craftsmen who had been associated with building the house. She called it Horestone *Cottage*, even though it could sleep fifteen people and had an immense dormitory at the top with large windows, sloping ceiling and rows of smallish beds. Gradually, the garden emerged from a field with its central lavender walk ending in a small paved square on which stood a sundial bearing the names of her brother Ronald and her two sisters Hilda and Janet.

My mother described the year 1928 as the happiest of her life. The years of bereavement had given way to years of growth and fulfilment, crowned now by the opportunity to build this house of her dreams. When she died, the stone was moved round so that her own name Margaret could face the house that she had created. The sundial is surrounded by rosemary for remembrance.

We children spent many happy days on the shore in a wooden Norwegian cow house which had been brought over in pieces and set up in a small cove facing the Seagrove side of Horestone Point. The cow house sheltered our canoes and sailing dinghies and a long concrete slipway took them into the sea. We changed for swimming on the roof of this boathouse with its traditional grass turf which in the summer burgeoned into a small hayfield. We lay there with the sun warming our backs, the soft scent of ox-eyed daisies in our nostrils and the grass tickling our toes. It was a time of deep pleasure and complete innocence.

As the 1920s drew to a close and my seventeenth birthday approached, I was still totally ignorant of, and in many ways unaware of, the opposite sex. The enthralling young man next door in Hampstead, Douglas Jay, had given me a hurried kiss, after which I seriously thought I might be in danger of having a baby and wondered how long my gym tunic could conceal my secret! Later, my mother told me there was *something* I must never do. I asked what it was and she told me I would know when I was married. When I was nearly eighteen, I appealed to a school friend for information on this mystery and then asked my mother why she had left me in such ignorance. 'But darling', she said, 'I allowed you to keep rabbits!'

CHAPTER · 3

The Boy Next Door

THE GARNETTS and the Jays had shared a garden fence for over ten years. When the Jay boys came home for the holidays from Dartmouth and Winchester, I watched them put up a shed or make a pergola for a splendid Albertine climbing rose with a quickening of excitement. Once our terrier broke through the fence and attacked the Jay's dog. I was then aged about fourteen and rushed through to disentangle them. But my interest in the activities next door was not echoed by the families themselves. Relations between the Garnetts and the Jays were cool. Once Mrs Jay included me in an expedition to the British Museum which I associate with measles – either I gave it to, or caught it from, the Jay girls Mary and Helen. I used to watch these two girls sitting at their high bedroom window having their long hair brushed by their old nanny Lizzie, who years later played such an important part in my own children's upbringing.

But by January 1929 my parents were concerned about my prospects in the forthcoming matriculation examination. They knew that the clever but impecunious young undergraduate next door (Douglas was by this time at New College, Oxford) would welcome the chance to earn a little extra money. They invited him and his younger sister, Helen, to stay on the Isle of Wight during the Easter holidays. This meant a welcome break for

Douglas from the strain of working for his finals in Greats. He was correct and careful with me during that holiday, clearly regarding me as a child, and the coaching as a job to be done – though he wasn't above playing hide and seek with us in the garden of St Helen's Cottage. But he made me break away from the sheltered life of beach and garden, teeming with young Garnetts, and took me and his sister Helen for long walks over the Downs at the south end of the island. When the exam results came out that summer, he wrote 'Splendid – you would have done much better if the exams depended not on memory but on intelligence like all the exams you will do in the future.'

On 28 January 1930 I was seventeen years old. That evening Douglas brought me a beautiful red and gold edition of Thomas Hardy's novels. With his wild dark hair and luminous brown eyes, he was more than ever an object of intense romantic interest to me. I can remember the exact spot where I saw him in his garden and thinking 'That man is going to be the father of my children.' He was six years older than me.

January 1930 brought not only my seventeenth birthday and the treasured Thomas Hardy books from Douglas, but also the birth of a new brother, Jan Nicholas Palmer (Jan after General Smuts, whose work my parents much admired). He was wholly unexpected. Indeed, my mother had informed me the previous August that she could think of no natural cause for this late addition to the family! I remember my mother and her friend Lady Layton, wife of the editor of the *Economist*, who had also just had her sixth child, being extremely piqued that they received not only congratulations but expressions of sympathy! None was needed. This latecomer was the apple of my mother's eye. Nicholas grew up a cheerful child, unambitious and un-neurotic, secure in his mother's openly expressed devotion. For me, it was a proud as well as a confusing time. Here was I, increasingly involved in my own romantic life, and there was my mother, having a baby. At seventeen I was past feeling the old jealousies, but the birth of this child removed my mother more than ever from me, at a time when I was much in need of a guiding hand.

In April 1930 Douglas's sister Helen died of polio, at the age of nineteen, after only a few days' illness. The family never recovered from the tragedy of her death. Only weeks beforehand she had heard that she had won a scholarship to Lady Margaret Hall. She and Douglas were very close, he had helped her with her work and encouraged her in the writing of her poetry which was later privately published. The shock and grief of Helen's death made Douglas abandon his plans for a fourth year at Oxford, including his work for an All Souls Fellowship, and he took a job on *The Times*. In that long, dark spring of 1930 there were many weeks of silence between us but by June there was a letter from him and in July we were playing tennis on the Foley House court. He decided, after all, to go in for the All Souls exam. Plans for him to work with me on my attempt to get into Oxford were also revived. 'Could we make it reciprocal?' he wrote. 'You will inspire my work as well as me assisting yours', adding the warning 'Getting into Oxford does not settle every question, in fact it raises more than it settles.' When in November he heard that he had been elected to All Souls he wrote 'You are partly responsible for all this' and again 'I am much prouder of you than of this fantastic gamble.'

At weekends during the autumn of 1930 I worked for my Oxford entrance exams in the ground floor front room of Douglas's home which was known as the library. We sat at a large Victorian mahogany table, surrounded by bookcases full of ancient leatherbound volumes – an early edition of the Bible from this collection now has an honoured place in the Winchester College library. Douglas took his task very seriously. 'If you can't learn to spell, it won't be worthwhile my even trying to get you into Oxford', he wrote and there were may adjurations to 'work all the time', 'to learn the facts'. He encouraged me continually as the dreaded day drew closer. 'You know plenty, if anything too much.'

After a day's work at *The Times*, Douglas would come back to Hampstead, from the office, at about midnight and throw gravel at the window of my turret bedroom in Well Walk. I would creep downstairs, praying that our chow, Chang, would not bark, and then, after laying an obstacle race in the hall against parental interruption, I would pass several intensely happy hours with Douglas in the sitting room. The only hitch that occurred in this enchanted life was one evening, when an aunt had been given my bedroom, I was elsewhere in the house. I had failed to warn Douglas of this, so when, as midnight struck, the gravel also struck the window pane, my aunt emerged in some annoyance. Seeing a shadowy figure in the front garden, she enquired if it were Mr Jay. 'No', he said. 'I never thought Fellows of All Souls told lies', she called down – and one evening of delight was lost to us.

By December Douglas was writing 'We will shoulder the sky' and speaking of lasting love, he quoted D.H. Lawrence 'She had known love and remembered passion. But this was neither love nor passion, it was the daughters of women coming back to the sons of God.'

As far as the daughters of women were concerned, Shiela Grant Duff and I were in constant correspondence when we could not see each other. She was still in two minds as to what to do with herself. 'I do not want to go to Oxford but I still feel something which may be conscience urging that step' she had written. 'Yes, she is a hungry animal, this goddess of Oxford' I replied, 'but she shan't have everything, her demands cut across all one's desires but I am sure it's worth it so long as we eventually meet in the city of the Gods.' I had not yet entirely convinced Shiela, however. 'You have never seen me properly' she wrote 'you have seen me only in my best moments, only when I'm trying to live up not only to your brains but to your morals

. . .' and in lighter vein 'Shall we be great politicians and clear away the slums . . . I'll be Disraeli and you can be Gladstone . . .' And then again, more seriously 'You're stronger than me – in every way, chiefly morally, darling, I am so horrid.' She was questing for the good and the beautiful. 'Perhaps all the beauty the war killed is somewhere – if only we could find it, if only we looked for it. People take all the misery, the suffering and hideousness the war has left and never seem to struggle to get away from it . . .' Finally, on a joint holiday in Cornwall I persuaded Shiela that Oxford was the right place for her, though she was still asking 'Is Oxford really on the side of the angels and poets?' I had never doubted that.

If I had any doubts, it was whether or not to get engaged to Douglas, doubts which I expressed to Shiela who wrote 'Don't go and throw yourself down crevasses or get engaged either to Rhodes scholars or Douglas Jay. I can't help you with DJ because I don't know him and all you tell me gives me a very conflicting idea of him. I think he sounds a nuisance . . .' So I decided I wanted the two people who were closest to me to get to know each other. 'I will do my best not to fall in love with her' Douglas wrote to me beforehand, just before his election to All Souls. And afterwards 'You are a glorious pair.' From that point onwards, the situation became increasingly complex. Without wavering in his feelings for me, Douglas wanted to include Shiela in them. 'I've had the most wonderful letter that ever was from Shiela' he wrote and told me.

In early January 1931 my parents gave a coming-out dance for me at home. Diana Hubback wrote afterwards 'It was certainly one of those especial dances I shall remember all my life – as I shall remember the lovely whirl of your white frills and the delicate youth of your flowers, smiling happily at one as one passed by.' And in a letter to Maire Lynd she wrote 'Peggy was a good hostess and a proper debutante, complete with gloves, bouquet and white frills – very happy cutting dances, mixing up her partners with abandon and looking radiant dancing the Blue Danube with Douglas.'

It was at this party that Douglas told me, while we were sitting on the stairs, that he thought monogamy was a sin. The starkness of this statement was tempered for me by an inner confidence that once we were married – though that was still on the far horizon – he would change his mind. So I said nothing. How little I really knew him to have such false hopes!

Shiela knew what I was feeling. She wrote me a wonderfully confidence-inspiring letter. 'It's not right that you should suffer so when you're young and Douglas is deadly cruel to make you. He doesn't realize what he's doing and he doesn't realize what you're feeling or he wouldn't do it. He still loves you, you are all that's left to him of the world he could have loved. To lose you would mean the end of the world. Go on loving him and help him because he is in great need of help and only you can give it to him – go on trusting him, too. He won't ever betray you. He may possibly think he's in love with other people, but it'll never be real or lasting because it will never be whole.'

But by September 1931 we were in very deep waters indeed. 'I know by loving and being loved by Dougle I am sinning in the eyes of the world but I appeal for its justification to something higher – the love of really great men like Shelley – but you are the arbiter, if you condemn it I suppose it will have to be altered, though the roots are deep . . .'

She was asking a great deal of me and sometimes I could not contain my wounded feelings, my temper got the better of me. 'Dougle has just rung up in a despairing way and demanded viciously to know what I've been doing to you' Shiela reproached me. 'Why did you go mad? . . . You're doing what you do so often, acting on false premises and total inaccuracies. You must not behave like that . . . it is entirely devoid of generosity or any finer feeling. . .'

I felt she was being rather hard on me. 'You have had an

appalling effect on him' I told her, and then, softening somewhat 'Sometimes I feel just a tiny bit that Douglas thinks he knows you better than I do ... You don't belong to him – write and tell him that.' In a respite from the emotional turmoil I wrote from the Isle of Wight 'I love my family so much and the sea is all blue and sunny.' But relations between Douglas and my parents were far from sunny. At one point, the strain was so great that I wrote Douglas a furious letter, suggesting we abandon our relationship. But I changed my mind and travelled up from the Isle of Wight to meet him. 'Dougle met me at Waterloo' I wrote to Shiela, who had remained loyal to our longstanding friendship, 'he was leaning against the barrier, so at first I thought he hadn't come. Having first ticked me off for having so much luggage, he then demanded that I should come with him to a dentist at Oxford Circus and wait while he had his nerve drilled. This I coldly refused to do having come home early in order to have tea with him at Waterloo. General fury and surprise. He dropped my luggage and said 'Well, find your own way home and bring some sandwiches, damn you.' He was obviously frightfully worked up and surprised and yet half expectant of my refusal to come to the dentist.

At eight o'clock I met a rather nervous but superficially arrogant Douglas outside *The Times* office. We slipped down the sinister little street to the river and climbed on the wall. He tried to keep off the subject of the letters but both of us knew that we couldn't be perfect until we had thrashed it all out. And so things were put right between us again, though I remember having written to Shiela even before this 'I feel as if my hold on the reins is being loosened, and sometimes that they are being pulled out of my hands altogether.' Indeed, both Shiela and I were sent on holiday to Brittany to get away from Douglas's influence over us. After Brittany, I moved on to Paris for a month, where I had a pleasant companion in Peter Floud, the son of old Hampstead friends of my parents, who was staying in the same pension in Bois

Colombes. Like me, he was about to begin his Oxford career and we wandered round Paris together full of plans for the future.

I wrote to Shiela about him 'He thinks a lot of the right things. Men have the capacity for seeing things much straighter than women. They are so much easier to talk to seriously. Peter is a teetotaller. He says everyone should be after a year at Oxford.' I loved his honesty and sincerity, and our friendship was a gently romantic one which continued throughout my years at Oxford. But whatever he may have felt, my heart was utterly and entirely lost to Douglas. I had just had a note from him after the news of my acceptance at Somerville saying 'I am so proud of you.' 'I love him so infinitely' I told Shiela 'I wish I could stop looking at myself as his possession (don't tell him I said that).'

So I went up to Oxford as involved with him as ever. What I had done for him was to open the door to a world of steadfast love which was new to him. For me, he had opened a door into a world of new friends. Without his devoted efforts, I should not have got into Oxford. Once there, his love letters which came daily for two years sustained me. I was not sure whether I should go up to Oxford officially committed to Douglas or not and wrote to my Poulton grandmother angling for advice. 'You *would* ask me such searching questions as to *when* a girl should become engaged!' she wrote back. 'When the right man comes along and the girl feels it is so and she herself knows her own mind, then I should say it would be the right thing to do ... Personally, I am always sorry when students come up here already engaged. They *cannot* possibly do such good work, nor can they enter into the life of the Society to which they go with the same zest and detachment.' Nor did Douglas wish me to be formally tied to him when I arrived in Oxford. In all sincerity, he wanted me to have the widest possible chance of friendships. He remained true to his own highest ideals, giving head and heart free rein to form new relationships, though he never allowed other romantic entanglements to detract from his loyalty to me. We did, in fact, feel committed to each other and spent all our weekends together.

By the Christmas vacation we announced our engagement in *The Times*, though Douglas was rather cross when I said I wanted an engagement ring. In the end, he sent me a letter to Oxford saying 'Here's ten shillings to buy a ring if you must have one.' I knew, of course that the pattern of convention was alien to him. He had committed himself to me fundamentally if not exclusively and I had to be satisfied with that. At any rate, after our engagement had been officially announced, the Dean of Somerville sent for me and said I could go to tea at All Souls unchaperoned.

The vestiges of the chaperon system still operated in 1931 but not with the severity of earlier years; students at Lady Margaret Hall had then to wheel their divans into the corridor at weekends when young men were allowed to call. It should be said that when I came up for my Somerville viva in February 1931 my grandmother and sister could not be dissuaded from accompanying me to tea at All Souls. But I firmly left them sitting on a chest at the bottom of the stairs while I went up to Douglas's room there to consume all his chocolate biscuits.

Now, without further let or hindrance I was able to enjoy meeting Douglas's friends, many of them young dons by then. Douglas wrote about Dick Crossman after I had met him 'I hope you weren't too hypnotized and fascinated by him.' Dick's immense physical and intellectual energy had made him a dominant figure in school at Winchester and undergraduate days at New College and there existed a longstanding love-hate relationship between him and Douglas. Dick was then a New College don living in a converted barn in New College Lane. He was newly married to his first wife Erica whom he had met in Germany. We regarded them as fascinating and so sophisticated, especially when he shouted down from upstairs to callers at the barn 'Come up, we're in bed.' On one wet walk with him over

Cumnor he said in his quasi bullying way 'If you hadn't already been involved with Douglas I should have married you myself.' There was no suggestion that this could be an arrangement in which the other person had a view! My papers still contain my laconic cards from Dick. One says 'Come if you like, ninny' and another 'Don't go in the canoe til I come' – the same canoe which Maire Lynd described to me as 'huge, green and beautiful. It took us one and a quarter hours to get up the river and ten minutes to come down, tremendously dangerous. Put off everything else and come.'

There was more than a touch of the poet about Dick and perhaps he was able to give expression better than any of us to the passionate idealism and idealist passions which made our Oxford days a time of hope and glory.

Out on the field under a quiet sky
The snow still lies in the furrows
White body leaning upon dark strength
But uncommingled –

Let not my clay contaminate your snow
Slipped from the upper firmament to discover
The secrets of your country lover,
But both lie easy til you know
The fastnesses of this wide frame you cover –
For then should winter soon be over
And corn stand high
Under a quiet sky.

Another friend of the early Oxford days was Goronwy Rees. He was elected to All Souls in the Autumn of 1931 at the same time as Quintin Hogg (later Lord Hailsham). Goronwy had been at New College and his first note to me was on New College paper. 'Will you come to tea with me on Wednesday, I've asked Shiela too. Would you like to meet some representative Oxford men? If so, what kind – political, aesthetic, moral, immoral or philosophical? Personally, I hate them all.' But they did not hate him. Goronwy in some ways embodied the longstanding love affair the English had with the Celts. His dark curls, humorous and impassioned flow of words, great sensitivity and intelligence took Oxford by storm. As was inevitable, Shiela and he became close friends. As did he and Douglas. We hoped to establish a kind of idealized quartet of all being in love with each other. Goronwy was an object of great envy and admiration because he had published a novel *The Summer Flood*. Some said the heroines were based on Shiela and myself. A letter from Vienna in early 1932 urged me only to 'indulge in what intellectualism really pleases you and not what others say ought to please you'. In the same letter he wrote 'I am surrounded by psychology and am a little bewildered among Oedipus complexes and homosexuality and incest and sadism but am relieved to find how little they mean when psychologists locate them in me and tell my why.' He said, however, that happiness for him must await his return to Oxford – which meant to Shiela.

The conflict between Douglas and my parents increased during my time at Oxford. He told Shiela 'I shall never speak to Peggy's mother again – she thinks the Edgware Road runs East-West.' Douglas's reaction was the enraged one of someone who thought in terms of unimpeachable precision, whereas that kind of literal accuracy simply did not enter my mother's scheme of things. What did concern her and my father was my growing involvement with this dominating young man. Inevitably, they wondered what his 'intentions' really were. Dick Crossman's report to Douglas that 'Peggy's parents do not think you will marry her as you are involved with so many girls' pretty well represented the views of many of the people who knew us. 'Even before we went up to Oxford' Shiela Grant Duff says in her autobiography *The Parting of Ways*, 'Peggy and I, barely eighteen years old, came under the rigorous barrage of Douglas's trained and first-class mind. It seemed at times as if all its fire was directed at disintegrating every value with which we had grown up and alienating us from the ideas held by our families, alienating us, indeed, from those families themselves.'

It is clear to me now that Douglas fanned the flames of revolt against parental authority, which were quite naturally rising in my adolescent heart and mind. He found himself in the role of intellectual freedom fighter liberating us from the chains of tradition and convention. This was particularly out of place in Shiela's case, whose mother was the embodiment of liberal-minded sympathy and support. However, even she was worried. My own parents, with their Quaker and Non-Conformist background, were more than worried, they were distraught. Their attitude to politics, particularly international affairs, was liberal and progressive. But their ideas about sexual morality were not 'advanced'. Engrossed as they were during the early 1930s with bringing up five young children, they felt their eldest daughter to be lost to them, swamped by the all-engulfing demands of Douglas Jay, who was adamant in his refusal to compromise. And so communication with my parents, who were simply not ready to cope with such a situation, more or less broke down.

Even before I went to Oxford, I had failed to live up to what they considered were decent standards of behaviour. One August on the Isle of Wight, when I was seventeen, I sunbathed in a backless swimming costume on the front lawn, visible to occasional passers-by on the adjacent country lane. My father called me in and told me firmly that to lie on the grass, in such a state of undress where I might be seen, was improper. He went on to suggest that I was doing it to attract the admiration of young men, a suggestion that provoked a hysterical outburst from me. Later in the day, my unhappy parents decided to seek advice from our neighbour, a woman specialist in psychiatry. She later told me that she greeted their anxieties with amazement, commenting wryly on the fact that my mother had herself appeared in a short dressing gown and bedroom slippers!

Fidelity and marriage, coupled with public service – based on a deeply held Christian faith – were the traditions that counted for everything, both in my family and in Douglas's. In his boyhood and youth, Douglas, with his father and elder brother, Alan, walked every Sunday morning from Well Road through Regents Park to All Saints, Margaret Street. His mother and sisters travelled on the bus. Sometimes the whole operation would be repeated for evening service. This restrictive regime at home, on the one hand, and the Winchester ethos of rigorous intellectual examination of every accepted social and moral issue, on the other hand, sowed the seeds of rebellion in Douglas. At home, he was looked on as a sort of God by his mother and sisters, his father taking a backseat, his attempts to join in a conversation frequently damped by a 'Be quiet Father!' from Mrs Jay. Such adulation had the effect of making Douglas rather conceited, sometimes to the point of rudeness. If a visitor whom he thought beneath his notice arrived, he would turn his back on them and talk to the cat. Once, when I was still at school, my parents tried to intervene in our plans to meet. Douglas wrote 'I am taking legal advice on the possibility of a kidnap.' During my second term at Oxford, things came to a head and my mother went to see Douglas's old tutor, our friend and mentor Christopher Cox. But her complaint that Douglas's retinue of young women made the whole thing seem like cats in the garden was laconically countered with 'Cats don't kiss'.

Of course, life had its lighter moments, too. One day when I came down to the entrance hall in Somerville to look in my pigeon hole for Douglas's daily letter to me – with *The Times* insignia printed on the back of the envelope – my very worst fears were realized when I saw that there was just such an envelope in every single pigeon hole, indeed, some had several. It took me some time to discover that *The Times* were circulating all new undergraduates!

My parents had prepared me rather inadequately for the

financial responsibilities of adult life. I received an allowance of fifty pounds a year but it was never clear what necessities this sum was to cover. They did, however, provide me with what I thought an exciting and excellent wardrobe when I went up to Oxford. Its chief feature was a splendid fawn velour three-quarter double-breasted overcoat with silver buttons which had belonged to my grandmother's coachman, an object of much admiration and envy. At one of the early All Souls dinner parties I had a scarlet velvet, what was then called 'picture frock', full-length, made by my mother's dressmaker.

My room at Somerville was over the main entrance facing onto the Woodstock Road. From the first day, I loved the college and the way of life, and made friends with Julia Pakenham and Prue Fischer Williams straightaway. Prue's father, Sir John Fischer Williams had been a distinguished international lawyer whom my parents had met, with his wife, when they attended the Reparations Commission in Paris in the early 1920s. I remember my mother telling me how Prue's mother had explained to her that her four young daughters could never go out alone in case their hair was cut off, a proper maternal fear as, with two blondes and two redheads, all with waist length hair, anything might have happened! Prue, exquisite like the Dresden china she later loved to collect, was the eldest of the four sisters. The next one, Jennifer, came to Somerville in my second year, gained a First, passed very high into the Civil Service and went into the Home Office. She married Douglas's great friend Herbert Hart. The third of the Fischer Williams sisters, Judy, came into our lives at a later stage. After Cambridge, she had married Eva Hubback's son, David. Their daughter, Camilla, met our daughter, Catherine, at the North London Collegiate School where, against all the odds of one's children liking one's friends' children, they became 'best friends'.

Julia Pakenham, statuesque with fair hair and blue eyes, was the chief of my Somerville friends. Her stable character and bright clear mind gave me great strength and comfort. She was the youngest of a large family brought up by a mother widowed in the war. She was the youngest sister of Frank Pakenham, later Lord Longford.

Another undergraduate friend was the exceedingly charismatic President of the Oxford Union, Tony Greenwood, later Minister of Housing and Local Government in Wilson's government. He invited me to the Union where we played uproarious games of hide and seek and sardines. Through Shiela, I got to know a handsome young German Rhodes Scholar at Balliol, Adam von Trott. Our old St Paul's friend Diana Hubback had introduced him to Shiela. He created quite a furore. After all, the end of the war was only just over a decade distant and a good many of us had never met any Germans. Adam was a proud patriot. A.L. Rowse, an Oxford friend of his, wrote to Shiela about him 'He gave himself up to Hegelianism; it profoundly affected his mind, though his mind must have been inherently predisposed to it: for all external appearances, Adam was deeply German. With him black was never black, white never white; black was always in the process of becoming white, white of becoming black.' Shiela and he kept in touch until the outbreak of the Second World War. In 1944 Adam was hanged for his part in the Stauffenberg plot to assassinate Hitler. Shiela's book *The Parting of Ways* was based largely on her friendship with Adam, and *A Noble Combat* published by Oxford University Press in 1988 is the collection of letters they wrote to each other between 1932 and 1939 which reflect those tortured, turbulent years.

There were family occasions in Oxford as well as those with friends. My second brother, John, was at the Dragon School while I was at Somerville and on Sundays I would sometimes collect him on my bicycle, and, with him astride the carrier, convey him to my room where I would feed him on crumpets, and he would help himself to Horlicks tablets which I kept in my cupboard. Once when we were out for a long walk with

Douglas, and little John was too hot in his overcoat, I made Douglas carry it. It seemed unnaturally heavy and we discovered that there was a Bible stuffed into one of the pockets, which led to even greater exasperation on Douglas's part. After a childhood of intensive High Anglican church-going, Douglas had rejected the whole shooting match even before coming to Oxford. This negative attitude, to matters of religion dear to my family, was a further cause of anxiety to my parents as they saw our relationship develop. In any case he was in their bad books on account of his unconventional sexual mores.

By the time I was a student, my Poulton grandmother was a member of the Somerville Council. From time to time the Poulton grandparents gave rather formal dinner parties which I somewhat reluctantly attended. Once, when there was a gap in the conversation, I said brightly that I had just finished reading D.H.Lawrence's *Sons and Lovers*. A frost fell upon the assembled company and later my grandfather told me, in stern tones, that I must surely be aware that D.H.Lawrence was not a topic ever to be mentioned in mixed company.

These occasions were a far cry from the candle-lit dinners, walks in bluebell woods and long conversations over cocoa – joys of my Oxford days from which two serious concerns emerged. One was involvement with my degree work, and the other, my growing political awareness and commitment. In my degree work I had a great deal of touching encouragement from the various young men. I had made a competent start in economics, but I was no philosopher. A note from Christopher Cox to Goronwy Rees about my intellectual progress described me as a 'harum-scarum creature of no intelligence'. Nevertheless, I got through Pass Mods, but it was decided I should do the Diploma in Economics and Politics, a two-year course, rather than the three-year Honours Degree in Philosophy, Politics and Economics which we knew as Modern Greats. I gained the Diploma and went down in 1933.

As far as politics were concerned, those of us with very early childhood memories of the First World War were reading Vera Brittain's *Testament of Youth*. This book, much of it written in Somerville, set fire to the dry tinder of our feelings about the tragedy and horror of war. The realities of Flanders had been more or less wholly concealed from the civilian population at the time; a relative's letter dated 1917 says 'I hear the men at the front all have colds, it must be due to damp socks in this rainy weather.' In addition, Robert Graves's *Goodbye to All That*, Remarque's *All Quiet on the Western Front* and R.C. Sherriff's *Journey's End* burst upon us.

I had joined the Labour Party in my first year at Oxford, influenced partly by Douglas but just as decisively by my League of Nations Union background. For the last ten years, my father had been stalking the country, speaking and writing on the principles of collective security, as a means of preventing future wars. His letters of the time are full of references to 'standing firm on Abyssinia, Manchuria and Japan'. There was no pacifism here, but a conviction that multilateral disarmament was the way to peace. He met with a good deal of discouragement in his work and I tried, in replying to him, to boost his morale 'I think it is so precious and wonderful to have a father who is an idealist, in the midst of this materialistic and cynical age. I loathe materialism and cynicism so passionately. Remember, Daddy, that the prophets of one age make the public heroes of the next' I wrote to him in 1932.

All this political ferment came to a head in the spring of 1933 when the Oxford Union debated the motion 'That this House will not fight for King and Country under any circumstances.' A letter I wrote to my parents described me as being in a 'tremendous state of political ferment' and how Tony Greenwood asked me to 'a party to throw Randolph Churchill into the river'. I was unable to get into the Union for the debate but remember vividly sitting on an outside Union window sill, from where

I could hear it all. Regrettably, I was clutching a dinner knife, I am not at all sure to what purpose! 'The majority vote supporting the motion will I hope show the world what the more intelligent members of this generation feel about war' I wrote at the time. My small brother, John, recruited thirty-five new schoolboy members for the League of Nations Union following that Debate. He told me he was happy to have found something about which he really cared and into which he could throw himself wholeheartedly.

But the Union vote was no triumph for pacifism, nor did any of us intend it as such. When I became a member of the Oxford University Labour Party in 1931, I joined a political group which hated nationalism and which was committed to internationalism and its shield, collective security.

In August 1933 I spent some weeks with friends of my parents in Bavaria, in the mountains south of Munich. They thought me strikingly like my mother when I arrived, but after a few days when we had got to know each other, decided that in personality I was more like my father. Hitler had recently been made Chancellor but it was easy enough to be lulled into a sense of false security by the peace and beauty of summer in the Bavarian mountains. I was full of plans for my marriage to Douglas, now only a few weeks away and enthralled by his letters which arrived with amazing frequency. So idle days passed, swimming, walking, picnicking with my hosts, who were not politically aware. But I was an avid reader of the British press which was divided as to what the significance of Hitler's rise to power might be for world peace. I was filled with hatred for this evil man from these early days and haunted by fears of another war, even though we had no hint of what the Nazis were up to in Munich. Sometimes, though, the silence at night was broken by rifle shots from the surrounding woods, sinister omens of the demented cruelties that were to sweep the country.

CHAPTER · 4

Fresh Horizons

ON 30 SEPTEMBER 1933 Douglas and I were married in Hampstead Parish Church. The September sun blazed down upon the reds and golds of the bridesmaids' bouquets of dahlias. They and the small page (my youngest brother, Nicholas) in their oyster coloured velvet complemented my oyster satin wedding dress. I felt supremely happy, supremely confident – this was what I wanted. Shiela, returning to a rather empty Oxford for her final year wrote 'Peggy has left to marry and settle down'. But I do not think this in any way describes what my feelings about the future were. I simply dismissed my parents' anxieties from my mind.

As far as they were concerned, the first crisis arose almost at once. When the friends and relations from both our families arrived at home in Well Walk, all set for the reception, the bridal pair had flown! I never faced the agonizing problem I left my parents to deal with – a wedding reception with no bride and groom to toast, though later I read some of the letters that came from their friends, offering comfort and reassurance over the strange situation. For the moment we got back from the church, Douglas announced that if we were to catch our train en route for Portofino we would have to make a dash for it. He bade his beloved cats a fond farewell and I changed rapidly into my check tweed going-away suit. 'Just the girl I want to be taking to Italy' Douglas said when he saw me in it.

We lazed in the magical blue of the Mediterranean, soaking up the autumn sunshine high on the cliffs above Portofino where Sir Thomas Bazely had lent us his house. Then we went on to the Tirol to Zell-am-See, a village high in the mountains on a lake, idyllic under unchanging blue skies and brilliant with flowers. In my eyes our honeymoon unquestionably reached the higher echelons of happiness. Later, Douglas told me that his honeymoon memories were overshadowed by the agonizing toothache that had plagued him until we found a local dentist to deal with it. After the Tirol, we stayed in Milan and one day, climbing to the roof of the Cathedral, we opened *The Times* to read that Hitler had taken Germany out of the League of Nations. Terrible memories of the First World War made my spine creep when I read this news. Throughout my childhood the League had seemed a bastion of safety against another war.

At the end of October we came back to London to our first home – the first and second floors of a terraced house in Paddington (now called Sussex Gardens). The large sitting room, with a view on to a splendid plane tree, looked restful with its pale walls and new limed oak furniture. We proudly possessed two small oil paintings which Douglas had acquired – one a Gilbert Spencer farmyard scene, and the other a lovely Roger Fry of a Cretan temple. The Thomas Hardy volumes Douglas had given me on my seventeenth birthday had pride of place on the bookcases which lined the walls. And yet, it was all rather unreal to me. I felt like a child playing at housekeeping, and couldn't understand why the gong didn't ring for meals!

I was catastrophically inexperienced in domestic matters, particularly the day-to-day routines of budgeting, shopping and cooking. On one occasion I lost my housekeeping cheque for two pounds ten shillings. Panic-stricken, I dashed into the bank and begged the cashier simply to *give* me the cash out of the kindness of his heart, as I could not get another cheque, since my husband was in hospital. No sooner had the words left my mouth than Douglas walked into the bank, bright and energetic! Once, at a dinner party Douglas suddenly asked me why other people's sprouts looked bright green while ours were always pale grey: I hadn't realized they needed peeling and washing. Douglas's mother used to send baskets of cooked food over to Paddington as she felt Douglas's health was suffering under my exiguous housekeeping. My cooking did not extend much beyond roast chicken so it was just as well Douglas's taste in food was generally recognized to be limited. At one of Dora Gaitskell's dinners, Douglas considered the tinned tomato soup the high point of an otherwise sophisticated meal.

Douglas had been at school and at Oxford with Hugh Gaitskell but their paths had not crossed. However, in the early 1930s they met on various Labour Party Committees. Later, in 1938, we dined with Hugh and Dora in the conservatory of a house where they were living near Swiss Cottage. It was the eve of the day on which Hugh was selected by the Leeds Labour Party as their parliamentary candidate following the death of their engine-driver member. He was elected and held the seat until his death in January 1963.

In the spring of 1933 Douglas had joined the *Economist* and worked hard with his colleague Geoffrey Crowther, for Sir Walter Layton, the editor, who was also Chairman of the *News Chronicle*. In the evenings and at weekends we gave many highly enjoyable parties when an ever widening circle of friends crowded into our flat. These included Nicholas Kaldor and Thomas Balogh, both newly arrived from Hungary. At our dinner parties we still practised the now abandoned ritual, of having the women leave the men in the dining room, to go and have coffee in the sitting room. Nye Bevan's prolonged reluctance to accept an invitation to dinner with us was due to Jenny Lee's refusal to dine with people where there was the slightest risk of the ladies withdrawing at the end of the meal, to leave the men to port and conversation. I always felt her assumption that women's conversation must be inferior to men's and therefore not worthy of her attention was hardly a tribute to her own feminist convictions. As far as I was concerned, after-dinner conversation with other women was often the most enjoyable and rewarding of the evening. At any rate, thank-you letters expressing people's enjoyment of these occasions flowed in, whether in appreciation of the roast chicken I managed to produce from my limited repertoire, or of the conversation. I'm not sure. For slightly grander occasions, we sometimes afforded outside help.

We had an elderly Vauxhall car whose supreme virtue was that its hood came down. This car took us away at weekends, to Oxford, where in January 1934 Douglas gave a twenty-first birthday dinner for me at All Souls; to Thomas Bazely at Hathrop Castle, to Lord Piercy at the Great House in Burford; to Nicholas Davenport at Hinton, and to John and Margaret Witt at Alfriston. But above all, I was enthralled and captivated by Douglas. We frequently talked about our concern for the growing menace of Hitler. On Sundays, we saw Douglas's family for supper. These were enjoyable occasions which, in fact, continued for the next thirty years. Douglas's father sat quietly with a humorous and reserved manner. His mother always changed for the evening and there was much teasing and joking with Douglas's sister Mary, who always took a very long time to heat the soup.

We also shared our summer holidays with the Jay family through the 1930s in a farmhouse on the North Cornish coast between Bude and Boscastle. This became very cramped indeed when Peter and Martin had arrived. Douglas's mother loved the Cornish coast, where she had been with her own children, during the First World War and the 1920s. Douglas's father used to come with us on strenuous expeditions down the cliffs and was also a great beach cricket enthusiast. I am ashamed to remember how little I saw of my own family at this stage. Douglas and I never visited them, though nothing could keep me from fleeting visits to them in the Isle of Wight.

My Garnett grandmother still held regular family prayers at Horestone Point right up to the mid-Thirties. Then this observance had to be abandoned, as she insisted on praying for the forgiveness of each individual's sins and omissions, including regular references to my bad temper.

Yet none of these things, neither Douglas, nor our social life, nor my token housekeeping, were enough to fulfil my youthful energies and enthusiasms. Douglas and I had joined the Paddington Labour Party and our friends Hugh and Ruth Dalton encouraged me to work for Haden Guest at his by-election in Islington. Early in 1934 I went to see Herbert Morrison and asked if I could serve on a Public Assistance Committee. He realized at once that my sheltered background in no way qualified me to understand or identify with the problems of family poverty and suggested I broaden my experience by joining the LCC School Care Committee organization. This had been founded by Douglas's father, Aubrey Hastings Jay, when he was Chairman of the LCC Education Committee, on the principle of voluntary work in the early years of the century.

It simply never occurred to me that I should do anything but voluntary work. No one during all my childhood had ever made a point of mentioning that someone had to *earn* what was consumed, and Douglas continued to pay the bills while I undertook increasing amounts of voluntary work. With hindsight, I see what strains this put on the marriage, with disastrous results. Ironically, on the day I left County Hall after thirty years unpaid work, an attendance allowance of ten pounds a day was introduced, an arrangement which would have transformed my life.

And so, based in an office in the Pentonville Road, I went visiting families, gradually gaining an insight into their needs and problems, which I reported at the children's school medical inspections. The dreary housing, the institutional prison-like, neglected buildings struck horror into my heart and mind. I remember standing in a public telephone box ringing Douglas, the tears pouring down my face as I told him it just wasn't possible for people to live like this and that something would have to be done about it. This exposure to the appalling inner-city conditions in the mid-Thirties gave my commitment to the Labour Party a determined swing into practical activity. Without in any way going back on my belief in internationalism, collective security and multilateral disarmament, as exemplified by the League of Nations Union, I now threw my energies into the battle against poverty. In our family we had always cared passionately for the underdog. I did not need to suffer deprivation myself to identify with the homeless families split up by the law's decree. The growing despair of the long line of outpatients waiting endlessly in hospital corridors and the heartbreak of a young mother separated from her child in hospital made me feel that it was *my* child crying in a hospital cot. It was this capacity to identify that was to be the driving force of my work over the coming decades. My reforming zeal stemmed from two apparently contradictory causes. On the one hand, the childhood feeling that I was one of the oppressed lived on in me and made me sensitive to others with the same sense of deprivation, whether psychological or physical. On the other hand, the spirit of idealism in fighting for just causes with which my father had inspired me, made me confident that if a job needed doing, I had the capacity to do it.

After eighteen months in Paddington, both Douglas and I felt a great need to return to Hampstead. We had enjoyed the break from our families, but now felt independent enough to risk living relatively near our family homes. We found a large, long flat on the top floor of a very ugly block at the top of Frognal. This flat showed off our goods and chattels to much greater advantage than the gloomy Paddington one and we loved it straightaway. The Gilbert Spencer painting, the clear lines of the bookcases and the oatmeal tweed of the huge divan were a great source of pride and pleasure. I remember Douglas's intense delight when he came home to find everything arranged and tidy after staying the night with his parents during our move and one of his ill-health crises.

On the whole, these were carefree days. There were the enchanting evening walks up Frognal to Judge's Walk and over the West Heath, as well as the charming lilac-filled route through little passages and up and down steps to the Hampstead tube and shops. Above all, we revelled in our independence away from our respective families. A friend had said 'Douglas only got married because his mother *would* talk to him at breakfast.' Douglas, of course, stuck to his dictum that monogamy was a sin, in spirit and letter. He flirted outrageously at parties – the Gaitskell's always ended theirs with dancing, and sometimes Douglas would disappear for hours on end. I did get very angry, but I was swept along on a strong tide of inner happiness and absorbing work and was able to pretend to myself that I neither knew nor cared.

During the General Election Campaign of 1935, Douglas and I worked for Hugh Gaitskell in Chatham where he was standing for Parliament, though he did not get elected that year. But we had our first taste of the campaigning and committee room routines which were to form so large a part of our lives. That year, too, as Douglas became involved with the inner workings of the Labour Party machine, on economic and social policies, we first encountered the grave and gloomy but immensely attractive figure of Leonard Woolf. His name was familiar to me as my father had often spoken of his dedication and longstanding efforts on behalf of the League of Nations Union.

As far as my work was concerned, it had not taken me long to realize that it was, in fact, the London County Council which was responsible for the schools and much of the housing in London and I became convinced that somehow or other I must become an elected member of that august and remote body. In May 1937 I was asked to stand as Labour candidate for the LCC. This invitation came as a result of my having been recommended to the LCC Labour Party panel by Herbert Morrison.

1937 was also the year that our first child, Peter, was born, and his arrival inevitably changed the direction of my life. When we were first married, neither of us wanted children. As far as Douglas was concerned, the essentials of the good life consisted in being free to work and to see friends without extraneous commitments. There was no place for children in such a pattern. He was also far too aware of the huge responsibility, and long-term commitment, that parenthood entails, to embark lightly upon it. As for me, I was thankful enough in the first two or three years of the marriage to be free of the clutter and claims of young children – my youngest brother was only three when I married. But by 1936 I was increasingly obsessed by the longing for a child. Moreover, it had to be the child of the man I loved, not just any child. After many discussions, Douglas finally agreed that we should have a child as I seemed, in his view eccentrically, so much to want one. Looking back now, I realize how much conversation with my contemporaries was concerned with how to prevent unwanted conception. In the years before the pill or the coil, the uncertainties of family planning were a constant preoccupation. Abortion was, of course, still illegal and so either highly dangerous or highly expensive. Thirty years later, the next generation have often been more concerned with how to *achieve* rather than prevent conception! When my mother heard that a baby was expected, she was far from delighted. 'I had so hoped for a longer gap between the last of my children and the coming of grandchildren – with no prams in the hall and no jam on the chairs!'

While I was expecting our first child, Douglas went away

for a skiing holiday in Austria with Shiela Grant Duff. I'm not quite sure what reaction in me she meant to evoke when she wrote 'I wish you were here. Your husband is really very nice, specially tonight when he is in the mood he has when he is rather tired and content'. I suppose I wished *he* were with *me*.

I had assumed that, like all my brothers and sisters, my baby would be born at home. As the date approached, however, my doctor felt it was risky to deliver a first baby in a flat at the top of eighty stairs with no lift. And so I went to the Belsize Nursing Home at the corner of Haverstock Hill and Belsize Grove, then a private nursing home which was later the maternity unit of the Elizabeth Garrett Anderson Hospital. I had a large, sunny, flower-filled room on the first floor – with a nurse all to myself. It was before the days of natural childbirth or epidurals, the old gas and air machine was on offer which I gratefully used. The woman doctor who delivered Peter was given a gold medal by her professional association for an article based on his birth. Peter's arrival on 7 February 1937 was a high point of happiness and celebration. This perfect baby, with fair skin, blue eyes and light downy hair, was the embodiment of all the heart could desire. Douglas arrived that evening with my mother, having established a temporary truce since they had not been on speaking terms for some time. Apparently, after having driven with her in her car to announce the birth in *The Times*, he had misdirected her in his over-excitement and they found themselves south of the river. Sadly, after this, my mother and Douglas remained entrenched in mutual antipathy.

Douglas concealed his pride and pleasure and said, on seeing his first-born, 'He looks just like a monkey.' He was certainly full of apprehension over the arrival of a baby. He must have voiced this to Shiela, for she wrote to him 'I do hope you do not resent the little thing too much.' My mother never spoke to me of her feelings about my longstanding wish to call this child Peter, after her own lost first-born son; nevertheless, I felt it pleased her. My Poulton grandfather wrote to me in characteristic vein '... Darling, you must not have quite such upside-down ideas of heredity! You did *not produce* Peter: you hospitably gave him his breakfast, dinner and tea, and gave him a warm comfortable home, but with these advantages he did everything for himself', and he then went on to give me a little lecture on Weismann's theory of the Continuity of the Germplasm. The letter ends with a sprightly postscript 'I saw *such* an attractive eighty-five-year-old cockatoo at the zoo yesterday.' The arrival of a huge, heavenly scented blue hyacinth 'For Peter' from Douglas's mother was a foretaste of the great part she played in his upbringing. When she was ninety, she told me that the last thirty years of her life that brought the grandchildren had been by far the happiest.

When Peter came home to our tall flat in Frognal Mansions, we got permission to put a south-facing window – in what had been our dining room – to make a nursery for him. There he spent two happy years, though looking back I am increasingly conscious of the burdens carried by a first-born – how much better I could have done it all! I was in my early twenties and far too impatient as a mother. I could not slow myself down to adjust to the endless need for repetition that young children thrive on. So I compare myself most unfavourably with my daughters and daughters-in-law, who embarked on parenthood in their thirties and forties and were much more aware that the stage of extreme dependency on parents passes only too swiftly. I was a novice mamma, grateful for the lifeline provided by the Hampstead Babies' Club run by Dr Oliver Plowright, in the Garden Suburb. I was tremendously reassured by his admiration of Peter's progress and would spend occasional afternoons sitting in our old open car with the pink straw Italian Moses basket in the back, the sun filtering through the trees in a road on the edge of the Heath Extension.

The arrival of Peter had brought me much closer to my own parents and family, though again I was out of phase. My brothers and sisters, growing schoolchildren, were not baby oriented, nonetheless, they found their new status as aunts and uncles intriguing. My youngest brother, Nicholas, aged seven, left a shilling piece under Peter's blanket when he first saw him in the Nursing Home. However, it was the friendship of Douglas's mother on which I became increasingly dependent. The Garnetts and Jays had agreed to have a small gate made between their two gardens in Well Road so that the pram and its occupant could pass between the two sets of grandparents.

Tolerant friends included our small Peter in their weekend invitations and we used to take him in the back of the ancient Vauxhall, tucked in his basket. One such Whitsun weekend in 1937 at the Pilkingtons on Boar's Hill, Oxford, was overshadowed for me by the delivery of a telegram for Douglas which our hostess flourished at him. It was from one of his girlfriends and said 'The first weekend in June is all right.' At this point, and for many years to come, I felt myself caught in a trap. I had agreed to Douglas's condition of a free and open marriage and therefore felt myself bound to avoid scenes of jealousy, but beneath a thin facade, I concealed great anger and deep sadness. I felt I had lost my bearings and sometimes, goaded beyond endurance, I relieved my always short temper by throwing this at Douglas. Though on the occasion of this particular weekend, all remained outwardly calm, I confided in Shiela 'Dougle has been putting his philosophy of love into practice with a vengeance ... I have found it harder not be jealous ... Dougle has always found it difficult to realize that one values passions and romance as much as loyalty and friendship. And he feels so long as he gives me the latter, one is not justified in expecting the former. I find this hard, being neither middle-aged nor unattractive. I wish I could understand promiscuity!'

Such confused and almost childish outbursts vividly express

the ignorance and inexperience with which I had embarked on marriage and which left me so immensely vulnerable. Later, when I was in a position to observe the young women of my daughters' generation, I realized how infinitely better prepared they were for the mature relationship of marriage. I had not had the opportunity to grow in self-confidence like my daughters and daughters-in-law, who had had jobs and homes of their own before marriage. They had felt free to engage in relationships with young men before marriage which gave them poise and balance and which I totally lacked. As far as I was concerned, marrying the only man I had known or loved, straight from home, was doing no more than exchanging one parent for another. Flinging myself into marriage at the deep end, as it were, I was defiantly determined to make the impossible work.

In the winter of 1937 Douglas was made City Editor of the *Daily Herald*. I remember boasting to the nurse, before Peter was born, that my husband had a wonderful new job that carried a salary of one thousand pounds a year. We had acquired some help in the house and I was able to work with the Care Committee in Islington on some half days. Hugh Dalton had written to Douglas 'I hope that Peggy is "obtruding her personality" (Mr Bevin's famous phrase) upon the London Labour Party office. I take for granted that the victory in North Islington was largely due to her successful canvassing.'

In the spring of 1938 the LCC member for Central Hackney died and a by-election was called. I was interviewed by the local party and clearly gave the impression of being even younger than my twenty-five years. At one point, the agent asked me if I could read an agenda – after the word *read* a burst of laughter drowned the rest of the sentence. This rather minor by-election aroused unusual public interest as it took place in the heat of the row over the LCC's refusal, under its leader Herbert Morrison, to allow their schools to be used for the meetings of the

Peggy, aged three,
and below, aged ten.

Shiela Grant Duff, Douglas Jay and Peggy in 1931 – our Oxford days (*by courtesy of Peter Owen Ltd*).

Wedding day, September 1933.

Engagement photograph, 1933.

In the garden at the Isle of Wight, 1938 – Peggy, the family dog, Peter, aged one, and mother.

The twins' christening at Hampstead Parish Church, 1945.

Martin, Douglas, Catherine, Peggy, Helen and Peter at the time of Douglas's by-election as MP for North Battersea, 1946.

(*Above*) Peter, Martin, Helen and Catherine at Seaview, Isle of Wight, in the summer of 1947.

(*Left*) Messing about in boats at Priory Bay, Isle of Wight, 1949. In the foreground, Martin and Peter, in the distance, Peggy, Helen and Catherine.

(*Opposite right*) Helen, Peggy and Catherine on Hampstead Heath, Bank Holiday, 1948.

(*Opposite below*) Helen, Virginia (Bottomley) and Catherine, as bridesmaids for an uncle's wedding, at St Helen's Church, Isle of Wight.

(*Above*) Opening Marble Hill House in 1964 as Chairman of the GLC Arts and Recreation Committee.

(*Left*) Peggy Jay as member of the GLC, and Chairman of the Arts and Recreation Committee, 1965.

Catherine and Helen on their way to meet Douglas at Heathrow airport, 1965.

(*Right*) With Peter, in 1976, at a reception following the Gala Spring Concert to celebrate the life and work of Benjamin Britten.

(*Below*) Eleven grandchildren blow out the candles on my seventieth birthday at Burgh House, 1983.

My seventy-fifth birthday at Burgh House, 1988, with Peter, Martin, Helen and Catherine.

A Hampstead party in 1989, putting the case about New End Hospital's re-development plans to Lord St John Stevas.

Joyce Jeal of the Heath and Old Hampstead Society presents Peggy Jay with flowers, on the occasion of the last AGM, after twenty-one years in the Chair.

British Union of Fascists. Hackney, with its high Jewish population, was a flash point. Fascist marches with men in black uniforms were loathed and feared by the local population.

Here, at the Hackney Town Hall in May 1938, was an occasion for a huge demonstration. Banners flew, crowds surged and chanted, mounted police cleared the way, as Herbert Morrison arrived to preside at this local eve-of-poll meeting. At his side on the high platform, gazing down into the packed hall, sat a young woman ablaze with the determination to right the social evils of poor school buildings and bad housing. I sat through this political baptism feeling neither fear nor diffidence, only concerned I should not be thought too young and inexperienced for what was being asked of me at County Hall.

I was safely elected. Douglas and my family were genuinely delighted. I had not considered the difficulties of undertaking more voluntary work while Peter was so small. All I knew was that I wanted both to do the work *and* to build a family. So May 1938 saw me as the youngest member ever elected at County Hall. The panelled corridors, sedate portraits and blue leather circular seats in the Council Chamber were my place of work. I served on the Education Committee and was dismayed by the lack of realism of many of the grave discussions carried on by my silver-haired seniors. My major concern was to see a building programme which would make the great Victorian schools fit for the twentieth century; to bring light, warmth, colour and comfort into these draughty caverns. I was horrified that children should often have to use lavatories that were doorless and roofless, exposed to cold and rain. But by 1938 the authorities were already thinking of how to counter the threat of war so that it was not a propitious time for suggesting these improvements. Increasingly, discussion centred on evacuation, sand bags, air raid precautions and the use of schools as centres for the homeless.

I remember a dinner party with Edwin and Bridget Plowden in Chelsea that year and discussing the possibility of evacuating wives and children to America in case of war. To my relief, Douglas spoke of cheery childhood memories of air raids in the First World War. I was always determined that I and the boys would *not* go to America.

However, even in that last year before the outbreak of war, it was possible occasionally to help people and I found the greatest satisfaction in the weekly 'surgery' in my Hackney constituency. London working-class life in those days was sustained by a network of neighbours, relatives and friends. The front door opened onto the pavement and meant companionship for young mothers and their children, as well as for the elderly. The support they gave each other could not, of course, counter the effects of extreme poverty and ill-health. The crowded houses made no concession to domestic labour saving: a shared cold tap down two flights of stairs was the norm. The mothers in the families bore the brunt of strain and overwork, there were no maternity or child welfare clinics, let alone family planning. Everyone was concerned to alleviate the appalling housing conditions of the inner city and thought all would be well if each family could have its own front door, bathroom and kitchen. In the Forties and Fifties, the planners and architects at County Hall interpreted this concern when they dreamt up the tower blocks. Little did we realize then that one evil had been substituted for another. The 'vertical street' became quite impossible for young families and the elderly alike – they suffered fear and isolation. Two or three decades later, the horizontal street has been rediscovered as a basis of neighbourliness and personal wellbeing.

One of Herbert Morrison's greatest virtues as a leader of the LCC was his willingness to promote able women members to posts of responsibility in the Council. However, in his authoritarian, paternalistic way, he had women past child-bearing age in mind. It was, therefore, something of a shock to him when I, a mother of an eighteen-month-old son, and another young woman, appeared in his ranks. At one party group meeting at

County Hall he was moved to ask that 'if lady members of the Council must have children, they do so in the recess'. So, obedient to his wishes, I planned the birth of our second child for early August 1939.

In the spring of 1939 we moved from our flat in Frognal to 42 Well Walk. Again we lived in a very tall, rather ugly red-brick Victorian house, set in a Georgian terrace. Next door to Number 42, the painter John Constable, his beloved wife and seven young children, had spent the last few years of his wife's life. Another historic link with the house next door was the memory of a very elderly friend who had seen Florence Nightingale sitting in a basket chair in the garden there. The great virtues of 42 Well Walk were its spaciousness and splendid views over London to the Surrey hills from the back windows. Our household was joined at this time by a young Wellgarth-trained nanny and a German au pair girl.

It was at this time, too, that my father retired and my parents moved to Oxford. They sold the lease of their Well Walk house to Hugh Gaitskell. Even long before he became Leader, I was always aware of his quiet strength and authority. Dora was the model politician's wife. She travelled constantly with Hugh and her loyalty to him was absolute, as hostile journalists learnt to their cost. As with other parents, children interrupted the calm of their domestic life, and I remember calling on them one breakfast time during which Hugh *implored* their smallest daughter to stop banging her spoon on the table.

That May, Peter, just over two, was brought home from playing in a neighbour's garden with the report that he had been sick. For several days he had a slight temperature though he complained of no pain. We asked our family doctor to call a consultant and a physician, Sir Alan Moncrieff, arrived from Great Ormond Street. His diagnosis was alarming, apparently Peter's trouble was centred in his lungs. I flew to the telephone and pleaded with Mr Twistington Higgins, a senior surgeon at Great Ormond Street, to come and examine Peter, which he agreed to do. Within minutes of his arrival, Peter was wrapped in a blanket and taken in the consultant's car to hospital. As we sat in the waiting room full of anxiety, Mr Twistington Higgins appeared to ask our permission to operate since the trouble seemed to be abdominal. After what seemed like an age, he reappeared to tell us that Peter had a burst appendix and advanced peritonitis. If he lived through the weekend, we might begin to hope.

Then began two weeks of hell. The hospital, in its wisdom (and this was 1939), decreed that I must not visit Peter, since any disturbance would be disastrous for him. So I paced the hospital corridors in the intense summer heat of that Whitsun with the tears pouring down my face, my second child due to be born within a few weeks. Calm and quiet, Douglas's mother *was* allowed to see Peter, and she became my lifeline. I have always felt that her special closeness to Peter was cemented in the long days when she sat by his hospital cot.

Many years later, however, when I, as President of the National Association for the Welfare of Children in Hospital, contributed to a correspondence the *Spectator* was running on this subject, a cheerful letter signed 'Peter Jay' appeared the following week, in which he said that so far as he knew he had never suffered any ill effects from not seeing his mother – while he was in hospital for two weeks – at the age of two! But whatever Peter thought about it, there was no doubt in my own mind that a searing personal experience had been behind my efforts to change the policy on the care of sick children. During the time of intense anxiety, Douglas's concern, support and practical help were beyond description and I was perhaps prouder of his comment in his autobiography *Change and Fortune* published fifty years later than of any other public recognition: 'My wife, to whose resource we owe his life, called in another specialist.'

In July, after Peter recovered, I was still dashing backwards and forwards by tube to County Hall for Council, Education and Parks meetings, though the new baby was imminent. I confess I found tremendous stimulus and comfort in my public work, not least when a burst of applause followed what I had said. This was particularly true on days when home seemed filled with disapproval. Applause from an audience made me feel I was emerging from the shadow into the sunshine. With hindsight, I realize that at this time I was trying to have my cake and eat it. Douglas felt he was being asked to shoulder heavier and heavier financial burdens while I undertook increasing amounts of voluntary work. With more hindsight, I think too, if Douglas could have given himself to the marriage more wholeheartedly, I should have spent less time in public work. But the seeds were sown for subsequent strains on the marriage. The birth of Martin in July, however, and the outbreak of war in September, temporarily shelved these problems.

CHAPTER · 5

The War Years

ON 18 JULY 1939 I missed the meeting before the recess at County Hall. It was, in fact, the last meeting before the outbreak of war, when the place was sandbagged and an inner group of senior members took over responsibility. I had been getting ready to go to County Hall when it became evident that more personal matters were to occupy me. Our second son Martin, large and dark haired, was born by tea time on that day, a day he shared with Julius Caesar, as our friend Professor Herbert Hart reminded me in his letter of congratulation, mentioning that 18 July was also *his* birthday.

I hastily summoned the doctor and nurse. She was at the hairdresser having a perm. Douglas had been speaking at a Hampstead Labour Party meeting and came in proud, almost despite himself, that Peter had a brother. I say 'despite himself' because I again sensed the ambivalence in him. On the one hand, he was proud and pleased to be founding a family. On the other, he felt intense regret that his life should be taking a course he had never intended. As he constantly reminded me, and I sometimes reminded myself, he had had children to make *me* happy.

From his earliest moment, Martin brought me immense joy. By the time he was two or three it was obvious that he had a great sense of humour which he used with enormous perspicacity to diffuse family tension.

In August, Douglas and I took our very small sons to Cornwall. We crowded into a farmhouse on the North coast above a sandy cove between Bude and Boscastle with Douglas's parents, his sister, Mary, and the Nanny. She, poor girl, found life primitive and difficult there. Matters were not made easier by Douglas's absolute insistence that he should not be woken before eight o'clock in the morning, a rule our new baby Martin frequently failed to observe.

At heart, Douglas and I were still very young. I remember a terrifying climb round the end of Cam Beak when, suspended by the strap of an ancient rucksack I saw the waves leaping eighty feet below and the dark, wet rocks towering eighty feet above. When we got back and boasted about our adventure, the farmer's wife asked 'Did you take the baby?'

It was in Cornwall that we heard the news of the outbreak of war on 3 September. It came almost as a relief to people of my generation. Since 1933, when Hitler had taken Germany out of the League of Nations, there had been a growing realization that only war would stop his maniacal nationalist ambitions. Later, in the Thirties, the knowledge of Hitler's persecution of the Jews and rumours of the concentration camps made a wider and more determined public opinion that he must be stopped. Munich had been a time of shame for wide sections of British public opinion. By 1939 there was no going back.

For the older generation, for people who, like my father, had been involved in League of Nations Union work, the outbreak of the Second World War must have seemed the ruination of all hope. Yet in fact, it was his organization which in the Twenties and Thirties had taught the world the ethos of collective security. In the schools, my father spoke on platforms throughout the country and it was he who coined the phrase 'World Citizenship' in the book he had written before the First World War which gave rise to the Council for Education in World Citizenship. The League of Nations Union also worked at governmental level with constant pressure on the Foreign Secretary of the day. My father remembered a deputation to Harold Macmillan, Foreign Secretary in the Thirties, when Macmillan himself recalled how ten years before *he* had been a member of a League of Nations Union deputation to the Foreign Secretary of the day.

When my father fell ill in 1938, the Chairman of the League of Nations Union Executive Committee asked for his resignation. Disagreement had arisen over the Peace Ballot. The whole issue of the popular front and Philip Noel-Baker's part in it was alien to my father's thinking. After twenty years of pioneering work, the circumstances of his leaving the League of Nations Union were tragic. Yet, though his grief must have been overpowering, my father never showed it, not even to his family. He was, in some sense, wrapped in a cloak of innocence and it was this that helped him to accept his dismissal without rancour. This innocence also covered relations with the opposite sex. His life-long exclusive dedication to my mother shielded him from the stresses and strains which so many people encounter in their relations. His vision of womanhood was focussed in the domestic setting created by my mother. He could not get on with the high-powered, articulate ladies involved in the transactions of the League of Nations Union business. By the time war broke out in 1939, people of my parents' generation never doubted it was a job that had to be seen through, whatever hardships it might involve.

On 4 September, the day after the declaration of war, a letter from my father had appeared in *The Times* saying, among other things '...we who live where liberty is held in high regard are not likely to emulate the dictator states in the use of propaganda. But if, as we believe, truth is on our side when we try to translate the fatherhood of God, the brotherhood of man and the unity of Western civilization into enough political unity to enable the human race to survive today's sudden changes in its material environment, it were madness to forego the help of so powerful an ally as truth itself. In Christian education, properly conceived, the world may yet find the best bulwark of a stable peace and the only sure foundation for world order.'

My heart went out to him and a week later I wrote home 'The Brave New World we tried to build after 1918 was within a finger's grasp of realization, the League and all that it meant all but succeeded – even now we were fighting according to the principles of collective security. One man alone has dashed all our hopes. But when Europe, and above all the German people, are rid of him, we can build again – but *never* while he is there. And I feel even if one is dead in the attempt, I would rather be dead and feel my children could grow up in a world where it would be impossible to live through again these ghastly years of fear, uncertainty and tension since Hitler came to power – than be alive in a world where that can happen again.'

Two of my brothers and eight first cousins were of military age at the outbreak of war and all of them served in the Armed Forces and survived.

The children and I went to stay with some elderly retainers of Douglas's family in Lympstone, South Devon. But by the end of September we were in Oxford, staying in my grandfather's house in the Banbury Road. He was very friendly and companionable in his last years – my grandmother had died before the outbreak of war. I am not sure how aware he was of the two great-grandsons occupying the old nurseries of Wykeham House. For Peter and Martin it was a first visit to a city which was to play a significant part in both their lives, at school and university.

Martin was christened in the University Church of St Mary's at the end of September. He looked exquisite in the Jay family's robes and ceased to be the focus of attention for a moment as Peter consumed a harvest festival apple from a window sill. The next day, my sister Pauline was married in the same church to Roland Hunt, one of the last men ever to be recruited into the Indian Civil Service. Peter was a page and escaped from the bridal procession to dash up the chancel steps. When confronted by the altar, he flung up his arms and gazed awestruck as a shaft of brilliant sunshine shone on his small blond head. He was removed through the vestry to sit with the chauffeurs during the rest of the ceremony. Roland left for Madras almost immediately after the wedding and Pauline followed him, sailing from Liverpool. I saw her off, saying heartlessly 'You know I shall be working for the end of British Rule in India.'

After much thought on Douglas's part and various stays in different places, we decided to join forces with Douglas's parents and sister. We found a modern house near Beaconsfield where the children and I spent two of the war years, 1941–43. The domestic quiet of life in Beaconsfield, walks in the neighbouring beechwoods, endlessly green, taking Peter to nursery school and dancing class, to some degree insulated me from the horrors of war. The beloved Jay grandmother and family friend, Lizzie, gave the boys a flying start. Lizzie had been with the Jays since Douglas's own childhood before the First World War and stayed with the family for over fifty years. It was Lizzie who saw to it that inevitable feelings of rivalry between the boys were speedily extinguished by tactful reminders that they loved and needed each other. Peter and Martin's lifelong friendship was forged in those Beaconsfield days. When I became a grandmother myself, I was deeply influenced by my children's relationship with their Jay grandmother, who had lived next door to us. The importance of the three-generation family in bringing up children is gradually being recognized again.

Douglas came down for weekends and I went occasionally to London. Then Lizzie would hold Martin up to the window to wave goodbye. I left, absolutely confident that both boys would be happy in my absence. Douglas was working in the

Ministry of Supply, with Oliver Franks and Edwin Plowden, on the recruitment of labour to man the munition factories. The culmination of my week was Saturday, when the boys and I went to the little railway station, to meet Douglas on his return from the hazards of life in London. I well remember the mounting excitement as we heard the throb of the approaching train. Douglas became a member of the local Home Guard and spent many nights on the tower in Penn Church.

In 1943 the boys and I moved back to 42 Well Walk in Hampstead. We were a busy, rather chaotic household with various wartime lodgers. They felt the basement of Number 42 offered a safe refuge from bombs; a feeling I thought illusory since the glass skylight at the top of the staircase would have given little protection against any bombs. But we did spend many nights in this basement. Once, smoke and a smell of burning filled the air, we were beginning to fear a gas attack when it was discovered that Douglas's feet resting on the stove in their bedroom slippers had caught fire!

Two of the people staying with us were Herbert and Jennifer Hart. Professor Hart was later President of University College, Oxford, but at this time he was working on highly secret preparations for the Second Front. His particular concern, of which, of course, we knew nothing at the time, was the plan to persuade the Germans that the landing would take place in the Pas de Calais and not towards the Brittany and Normandy beaches. Jennifer, who had been a friend of mine at Somerville, was in the Home Office.

Another wartime lodger was Sir Christopher Cox who had been Douglas's tutor at New College and a confidante and adviser to Shiela and me in the Thirties. He was the archetypal academic bachelor, wise and unstinting in his affection for generations of undergraduates. He was one of Peter's godfathers. He organized many hard-working, hard-playing reading parties in North Cornwall, but dearest to his heart was the chalet New College owned above Lake Geneva. It was Christopher's responsibility to organize the reading parties there. Apparently, when he was dying, it was to this spot that his thoughts turned and his last moments were occupied with making provisions for it.

My mother had had the initiative to set up a community kitchen, one of the great features of wartime life, in her Park Town garage in Oxford. It widened gastronomic experience in a most enjoyable way. In Hampstead, the boys and I much appreciated the British restaurant in the Salvation Army Hall in Flask Walk which provided an adequate two-course meal. Rationing, as far as I was concerned, eased domestic arrangements. It gave me pleasure to produce six ration books and leave the amounts of each food which one was permitted to have to the shopkeeper. I always carried a briefcase rather than a basket on my shopping expeditions, even if the briefcase only contained a loaf of bread, an indication, no doubt, of a certain identity problem in the double strand of my public and private life. Our household now also included a dear elderly lady, Miss Lennard, who did evening babysitting. She loved the little boys and they her.

My work life consisted of flying visits to Hackney, which I reached by the same Broad Street line that had taken me to school years earlier, though now I was travelling in the opposite direction to Dalston Junction. County Hall was still more or less closed down, but the constituency work continued and my chief concerns were the problem of housing, evacuation and air raid damage repair. These were times of high tension in which a new awareness of the fragility of life made each day lived a day gained. I vividly remember the warmth of Douglas's welcome as I came back home through the door from evening meetings. In 1944 new mystery missiles which proved to be the V1s and V2s became evermore threatening and we tried to spend more time out of London.

The Isle of Wight was a haven of peace and refreshment. As this was a highly secure area from the military angle, we were able to reach it only by dint of a much worn letter from my grandmother who lived in the island, saying she urgently required to see us. I also saw something of my brothers, Michael and John, who were in the Army and Navy respectively. John was involved in highly dangerous and secret work based at Falmouth. As an RNVR lieutenant he was in charge of a small French fishing boat which would lie up in the Scilly Islands while they transformed themselves into French fishermen and headed for the Brittany coast, where they rescued British agents. In one case on a Christmas Eve, these British agents were waiting up to their waists in water at midnight along the rocky Brittany coast. Contact with my sister Pauline, in India, was kept up through an active correspondence on flimsy airmail letters which kept her in touch with life at home. My sister, Priscilla, and young brother, Nicholas, were schoolchildren during the war.

Shiela Grant Duff was working in the European Section of the BBC and we met frequently. She had married Noel Newsome, a colleague at the BBC, and they were living at Stoneleigh Abbey with their small children. Later, with her second husband Michael Sokolov, she took up farming in Northumberland and in Suffolk. She worked hard in the role of confidante and conciliator when my relationship with Douglas became increasingly stressful.

Diana Hubback had married David Hopkinson and was living in Wiltshire with her young family. Julia Pakenham, who had married Robin Mount, was also living in Wiltshire, in Chitterne. When I went to see these friends, our conversation was centred on the desperate times through which we were living. Shiela had lost a brother at Dunkirk, Diana Hopkinson's husband was in the Eighth Army. Ruth Adam, my friend of pre-war Hampstead days was deep in the country, in a rectory in Kent surrounded by nettles. The boys and I stayed with her on two or three occasions and I realized how exposed Kent was from the point of view of aerial warfare. Ruth was discovering her writing talents and later published several novels, giving a picture of wartime life on the home front.

Hugh Dalton invited us to his country house in Wiltshire. 'There'll be little to eat, a bit more to drink, no hot baths and *almost* no shop; just the Downs and a lot of sky. Good walkers only are invited here.'

It was during a wartime visit to All Souls that I first met Harold and Mary Wilson. They were engaged and I remember her saying how delighted she was to becoming a don's wife and living in Oxford, as she particularly disliked any form of public life, above all London! The Wilsons' early married life was spent in Jesus College. Elderly bachelor dons were amazed to see a pram and nappies on a washing line in a distant quad.

In May 1944 Peter, aged seven, who was at school at Byron House in Highgate, announced to travellers on the 210 bus 'I know where D-Day is going to start from.' This alarming statement was based on his observation of the crowded lines of shipping as we crossed the Solent for our Easter holiday in the Isle of Wight. I remember walking on the Heath with Douglas and his brother, Alan, in the June of that year and noticing how constantly and anxiously they gazed at the sky and how clipped words about the weather passed between them. It intrigued me later to realize that these were the crucial hours in which the D-Day operation had had to be postponed because of the weather and that I had been in the company of two people who knew the situation, but inevitably said not a word either to me or to each other.

In June 1944, Number 12 Well Road, next door to Douglas's parents, came on the market. 42 Well Walk had become too large and unmanageable, despite the presence of friends as wartime lodgers. My mother came from Oxford for the day and bought Number 12 for two thousand pounds. The forty-year lease seemed like perpetuity. Despite occasional air raids and the threat of unknown secret weapons, we moved into Well Road in high spirits. The small sunny garden where Douglas always breakfasted and the tall friendly house provided the perfect setting for our rather ramshackle family life. Quite apart from wartime shortages, our very restricted finances meant ragged stair carpets, chairs and sofas with exhausted springs and no labour-saving devices. It made an ideal home for small boys since there was nothing to spoil. Douglas, working all day and most of the night at the Ministry of Supply, was something of a fleeting figure, though he always had time for the boys and joined wholeheartedly into their activities, whether it was building with bricks, playing with railways, cricket, or going for walks. During our short wartime holidays in North Cornwall he relived his own childhood, climbing rocks, playing beach cricket, swimming in the surf and organizing long expeditions along the cliffs. Those early days built the foundations of Peter and Martin's lifelong friendship with their father.

In the summer of 1944 a V1 fell on the edge of the East Heath at the end of Well Road. Crouching under a bed on the ground floor, the boys and I heard the considerable explosion which made the front door blow open and the ceilings crash down on the staircase. Martin, aged four, announced 'That is the best Blitz we have ever had!' At that moment, Douglas, wrapped in his vast Jaeger dressing gown, entered the room proclaiming 'If all this noise does not stop, I shall not be able to go to work tomorrow!' We found a twisted piece of metal from the V1 on the Heath next morning. It is now in the Burgh House museum.

Douglas's parents had also returned to Hampstead and his mother was enjoying her grandsons, taking Peter and Martin for walks on the Heath and providing regular teas in her drawing room with the ritual of silver teapot, hot scones and coal fire. This tradition provided the boys with a thread of continuity in the turmoil of a war-torn world. The support I had from

Douglas's mother and her devoted housekeeper Lizzie, in the house next door to ours, is beyond estimation.

In the autumn of 1944 there came a strange interleaving of personal and public life for me. Though I had no ambition for a repetition of the six-child family from which I came, I had always felt that two children were not enough to call a family. To my great joy I found a third child was on the way. And this when I had just been appointed to the Royal Commission on Population! Little did those who appointed me realize that I was very soon to become the mother of identical twin daughters.

The Commission was appointed after growing anxiety about the fall in family size. The actual birth rate stopped falling in 1933. Anxiety, however, focussed on what some regarded as the collapse of the middle- and professional-class birth rate. Eva Hubback, then Principal of Morley College, had published a paperback entitled *The Population of Great Britain* in the late Thirties. It was in this climate of opinion that we were appointed. I felt a certain sympathy for our chairman Lord Simon as he threaded his way through what was at that time a minefield of forbidden and unmentionable subjects. I recall the day on which, with strangled voice, he announced 'Today we have to discuss the distasteful subject of abortion.' I said cheerfully that I did not think we should make too heavy weather of it as there was probably not a married woman member on the Commission who had not experienced it. I have to say that the next month Lord Simon retired and Sir Hubert Henderson took over.

We met in the Moses Room of the House of Lords, a place of grave beauty, with its massive windows facing onto the river. Our discussions were often interrupted by air raids. We would hear the sirens, the rattle of anti-aircraft guns and the crump of falling bombs. When House of Lords messengers opened the doors to announce the raid, we continued with calm. On only one occasion did we crouch beneath the heavy mahogany table.

Of the other women members on the Commission, Lady Ogilvy was my closest friend, but it was, in some sense, the Civil Service in the form of the Secretariat with which I had the closest links and correspondence. Huge wads of evidence given to us by various organizations were circulated for discussion at ensuing meetings. Later, many of these people came as witnesses to be questioned on their attitudes and proposed solutions. Eva Hubback was a great strength to me in this field. I would take the papers over to her at weekends and we would go through them. She had been the inspiration for the creation of the Commission though she was not a member of it and I like to think that these discussions gave her a sense of close involvement.

The coming of our third child caused Douglas, and therefore me too, in spite of my initial delight, immense anxiety. After interminable arguments I went for counsel to Dr Joan Malleson with Douglas. We visited her on a freezing evening in December 1944. Her skilled advice and warm friendship brought peace of mind to both of us. I have often asked myself whether, even at this very early stage, she diagnosed twins. Be that as it may, Douglas and I walked to the bus stop clasped tightly arm in arm against the east wind.

When I was on the Isle of Wight for the Easter holidays in April 1945, I had a letter from Eva Hubback saying 'I have heard of your expectations. Twins are such an achievement, and such fun. Do you want identicals or fraternals – the latter are three times more frequent than the former – one girl at least, I take it, is required.' My family thought that I must have got the dates wrong. They thought it impossible I should have to wait until June for the birth, so the local doctor arranged an X-ray (which I still have) and there, to my joy and amazement were the two perfectly formed infants tucked heads down one with the other. I did, however, suffer some shock when the doctor told me the babies were still very tiny and that I would have to hang on to them for another two months. They were two peaceful months in the Isle of Wight Nursing Home. Peter and Martin returned to Hampstead for the start of the summer term at Byron House School. Gran Jay and Miss Lennard between them organized their lives.

I lay comfortably, remembering how only three months before, at the end of January I, with young Martin dressed in a green baize suit made out of a kitchen tablecloth, had leapt from the end of Ryde Pier into a naval packet boat to get to Douglas's brother's wedding. All ferries had been cancelled because of the winter gales. When I called to the boat to ask if they could take us across the reply came 'Yes, if you can jump'. So jump I did. My brother-in-law Alan had for months been involved on the Murmansk-Archangel run, protecting shipping from German submarines. He was later responsible for mine-sweeping operations in connection with D-Day. Later still in his career, it was he, as Prince Philip's commanding officer, who had to grant the Prince permission for leave of absence for his wedding.

VE Day came while I was in the nursing home and, since I had listened to every radio programme over the war years, I realized quite fully the greatness of this day of achievement, on which thankfulness for survival mingled with national pride. My reading included *David Lloyd George's War Memoirs*. When the twins arrived with the minimum of trouble on 18 June they fulfilled all my mother's requirements who had wished for 'female, blonde and beautiful' babies. At over six pounds each, they were welcomed with flags on their grandparents' Oxford house. I had agreed with the Population Commission's secretary to send a telegram when they were born. If boys, the message was to read 'Two contributions to the reproduction rate'; if girls, 'Two contributions to the *net* reproduction rate'. So when Douglas returned home from work on the tube that day, he was amazed to see the headline in his neighbour's evening newspaper above a photograph of me. 'Two contributions to the net reproduction rate.' Douglas's note to me said, 'Statistically it is certainly very good. It never rains but it pours.'

Next day, he came to visit me on the Isle of Wight. I was very conscious of his reservations about the new daughters and noticed he sat very near the window as if ready to make his escape. While I, at the end of months of strain, was relaxing in pride and joy over these lovely babies, he was only too desperately aware of the financial and other implications of his increased family. When we were choosing names, Douglas insisted they must have a basis in Latin. Some people thought they were named after the two Isle of Wight saints St Helen and St Catherine. In fact, the elder was named after Douglas's much loved sister Helen who had died so young; and I, with my enthusiasm for *Wuthering Heights* had always wanted a Catherine. Thirty years later, Catherine called her own daughter Emily in tribute to the Brontë name. The boys, who treated the arrival of their sisters as something of a joke, reacted in their different ways. Peter said 'What a shock for Daddy' and Martin 'Good, one for each of us'. And so it proved to be. Helen turned out to be Peter's, and Catherine Martin's, special companion.

My sister, Pauline, helped me bring the babies from the Isle of Wight back to London. Douglas's mother and Lizzie met us at Waterloo. As Lizzie gazed into the Moses baskets, I heard her say, looking at Catherine who was the smaller of the two, 'Mrs Douglas will never rear that one.' Thus began a hectic time, though in a sense twins bring their own help with them. We had a Danish au pair and extra pairs of hands came from the house next door. Once, when I had pushed them in their large twin pram up to Highgate to fetch the boys from school, Martin rushed out and showed the babies off to his small friends. One child said 'Look, two heads'. 'Yes,' said Martin, 'no legs, no legs.'

So, the war was over. I have always felt that for England the Second World War was less terrible than the First. Civilian populations were able to some extent to share the burden with the Armed Forces. With vivid memories of the appalling and unnecessary sacrifice of life from the First War, political leaders were determined on much more careful planning. As far as my family was concerned, for instance, three of my uncles were killed in the 1914–18 war. In the Second War, I had two brothers and eight first cousins in the Armed Forces. All survived. For Douglas and me the war years were, on the whole, a unifying period, each valuing intensely the other's survival and each confident in the justness of the causes for which these enormous efforts were made.

CHAPTER · 6

Labour Years

IN OCTOBER 1945 Labour won the first post-war General Election. It was the fulfilment of years of hard work and campaigning during the 1930s. Douglas and I knew how ideally Attlee was suited to the work of reconstruction and peacemaking. Through his work for the Labour Party, Douglas had come into close contact with Attlee and admired his quiet manner, his keen, clear mind and his concise way of expressing himself. Douglas had first come across Attlee as long ago as 1917 when he was a schoolboy; one day when he was coming home from church with his family they met their neighbours, the Millars who lived next door in East Heath Road. A young man was with them, dressed in breeches and leather gaiters. The daughter Violet introduced him as her fiancé Major Attlee.

Douglas and I took a short holiday in Postbridge, in the middle of Dartmoor. One morning while we were there, the telephone rang and Douglas was summoned to Downing Street. Late on the afternoon of the next day, I set out to meet him. As I got to the crest of the moor, the road reaching into the evening mist, I saw him coming. He had been appointed Attlee's adviser on economic matters and so, in great joy and excitement, began his longstanding association with Number Ten.

Douglas entered into his new work knowing that both he and the new PM identified with the needs of the underprivileged. He was also confident that the senior civil servants with whom he would be working were 'reasonable and straightforward beings'. As he has said in his autobiography *Change and Fortune*, he felt that the Labour Party's 'inferiority obsession' as, for instance, exemplified in Marcia Falkender's book *Inside Number Ten* that senior civil servants were 'sinister and hostile', was an unfruitful and unrewarding attitude.

These were days of high hope. No 'Lend-Lease' with its dollar and balance of payment crisis, not even fuel shortages or the world goods scarcity, could dampen the exhilarating sense that a new era was dawning. As I looked across the river from County Hall to Westminster, I realized that our purposes and plans coincided exactly with those of the new Government. Herbert Morrison had become Home Secretary and thus a senior member of the Cabinet.

Douglas was elected to Parliament in June 1946. The twins made a very attractive cover for Douglas's election address with their blonde heads and white smocked dresses. After nearly ten years of Council campaigning, the by-election was something I could take in my stride. I was used to being buffeted by arctic winds on the high balconies of tower blocks, to having the door slammed in my face, to being invited for the occasional cup of tea. The uncertainty of one's reception heightened the tension, but the June 1946 by-election was sunshine all the way.

In 1946 Peter was nine, and Martin six. Martin always maintained he had no time to learn to read at Byron House in Highgate, he was so busy climbing the lilac tree or hiding in the depths of the rug box. When he was eight, his energy and enterprise caused family amazement and anxiety when he announced that he had cycled (on a very small bike) all the way to St Albans and back. Certainly, he was very dirty, tired and hungry and had disappeared for several hours, and there was no doubt that he had done something remarkable. We were both proud and also frightened.

In September 1946 Peter went as a boarder to the Dragon School in Oxford. This was quite a strain on us financially, we got second-hand uniform, some from his young uncle Nicholas. My parents were living in Park Town in Oxford and I often stayed with them to reassure myself of Peter's well-being. Years later, he told me that life at the Dragon School in those early years was tougher than anything he experienced later, even including his time during National Service in the lower deck of the Navy.

A photograph of Helen and Catherine's second birthday party shows them by their cake with Goronwy Rees's twins, Helen Cohen's twins, the Gordon Walker twins, Geoffrey Durbin, Freydis Murray and Alice Fairfax-Jones, all aged two or three. In infancy and early childhood, since the girls were identical, there was occasionally a problem even for me of knowing who was who. I remember calling to one of them as she came down the stairs aged three 'Helen!' 'No', said Catherine, 'It's not me'. Though as they grew older they became increasingly different both in personality and appearance, they would still, even in their forties, sometimes appear at parties dressed uncannily alike. In later years, Helen and Catherine both felt that I had been too preoccupied with outside work during their early years – more so than my contemporaries the Plowdens, the Crowthers, the Wilsons and Ruth Adam, who all spent more time with their children. Even so, though of course work at County Hall took time and energy, I was at home much more than I was out. On one occasion I rushed into the house intent on being home before the girls returned from school, to hear Helen saying on the telephone 'No, Mummy's not in. She's out giving a talk on the importance of mothers being home when their children get back from school.' I recall a teatime in our Well Road kitchen when Catherine steadily poured the contents of a two-pound tin of golden syrup onto the floor as she concentrated on our conversation. I simply sat back and laughed, feeling refreshed and good-tempered after half a day's work at County Hall.

Douglas's attitude towards the children was a mixture of humorous toleration and ferocious devotion. The former was exemplified when Martin, aged seven, built a fire on the floor of his playroom and burnt a hole in the linoleum. I appealed to Douglas for reprimand. All he said was 'I always told you not to have them!' I myself was very far from being cushioned by private recognition and encouragement which many people feel to be an essential concomitant to the stresses and strains of public life. Douglas tolerated my work, but only just, nor was I ever allowed to have an inflated view of myself. Sometimes, as I dashed to the tube in my bright red coat I felt that I was coming out into the sunshine of approval in my public activities, after the sense of disapproval which I felt at home.

Round about this time I had a letter from Shiela Grant Duff on the vexed question of where a woman's place was. It was inspired by Douglas, but its tenor did rather surprise me, coming from Shiela, who had been very much a career woman. 'I feel challenged' she wrote, 'when Dougle says "It's amazing that even after thirty years of the vote women haven't yet reached Cabinet rank". But I think it's a wrong challenge.' She went on to say 'It's time to recognize that socialism has destroyed feminism and to think out again what is the function of women in modern society. If it's no different from that of men, then there's got to be another revolution – the destruction of home life. Children will be brought up by the state and personal relationships will be built up and maintained in public places. I think rather than that, I would submit to the thesis that a woman's job is to make a home and that her influence on affairs must primarily be indirect i.e. through her influence on her husband and friends.' These are problems which even today, in the Eighties have not been solved, although there *is* a fundamental change in the attitude of young fathers towards the sharing in the bringing up of their children.

In July 1948 Catherine, aged eight, was rushed into the National Temperance Hospital with pneumonia, which she developed after measles. When we got to the hospital I followed as she was carried into the ward and put to bed. I sat down on a chair beside her. At this point a succession of indignant hospital staff informed me that visiting was twice a week and would I come back in two days' time. I was not now the submissive, frightened young mother who ten years earlier had been excluded from her son's bedside. As increasingly senior staff urged my instant departure, my resolve to stay was strengthened. Finally, I told the consultant that he could call the police or sue me for trespass, but that he must surely know that the only place for a mother with a sick child was by its side. After that I was left severely alone and came and went as I wished. Some twenty years later, in the Seventies, Catherine's daughter, Emily, was gravely ill following a heart operation at Great Ormond Street. Her parents, and indeed myself, were made warmly welcome to spend hours at her cotside. A revolution in the attitude of hospitals to child patients had quietly taken place. I would claim that this was largely due to the work of a small group of young mothers in Battersea who founded a pressure group to become known as the National Association for the Welfare of Children in Hospital. Their purpose was to see that every children's ward in the country put into practice the recommendation of the Platt Report on open access for parents of child patients. This group now asked me, as the wife of their MP, to become their first President.

Early in September 1948 when Catherine had recovered, Douglas and I and the four children were on holiday in our familiar farmhouse on the cliffs of North Cornwall above Crackington Haven. Our friend, Evan Durbin, was holidaying with his family and friends in a nearby cottage. On 3 September, a day of westerly gales and high seas, we were down on the

Haven beach when news came that Evan had been drowned on the Strangles beach while rescuing his daughter's friend. Douglas and I flew along the cliffs, only stopping to take a long rope. As we reached the cliffs above the Strangles we saw Marjorie Durbin standing alone. Quietly she told us that there was nothing we could do. Evan was lost. We raced down to the beach and spent a long time searching, but though we were so familiar with the place, and I was confident that we would be able to do something, we came away defeated. The procession of black Government cars (Evan was Minister of Works at the time) making its way down the steep Cornish lanes and passing our door is etched on my memory. His death was not only a terrible loss to Marjorie and her children, it also hit Hugh Gaitskell hard. Sitting behind Hugh at Evan's Memorial Service in St Margarets, I was aware of the intensity of Hugh's feelings. He had lost a personal friend and political ally and would henceforth stand alone in high places.

Soon after the war, my mother felt that the pressures of housekeeping and disturbed nights with young grandchildren in the Isle of Wight house were too much for her. She suggested to my brother, John, who had married Barbara Rutherford Smith in Chester Cathedral in 1941, that he should convert the wooden Norwegian cow house, which he did with great flair. Perhaps his greatest achievement was the building of the huge logburning hearth with its chimney of local stone. It was the creation of this family home during the Forties and Fifties which meant that I saw much of him and his family. The eldest of their four children, Christopher and Virginia, were the same age as my twins, Helen and Catherine. Churchgoing in my adult life became closely associated with Isle of Wight holidays. It gave me great pleasure to go with the rest of the family to the little Parish Church across the fields. There certainly was a special rapport between John and me, I always felt better and stronger after a few days in his company.

Although I was deeply involved in party political affairs and he was not, we shared a basic radical liberal approach to public affairs. He was able to give full expression to this when he was appointed director of the Industrial Society after he left ICI. This Society was founded by George VI as the Industrial Welfare Society and was based on the then King's great concern for developing mutual understanding between employers and employees. By the Fifties the Industrial Society had become a nationwide organization enabling employers and employees to meet in conferences and seminars and so to improve the climate in labour relations.

By the late Forties, the Labour Party was already showing signs of division. This was reflected in the House of Commons and, indeed, in the Government. The groupings were broadly represented by Aneurin Bevan, Richard Crossman and Harold Wilson on the left of the Party; Hugh Gaitskell and Douglas to the right. The scene for conflict was set. After the LCC election I had talked to Douglas about the anxiety of many women following Aneurin Bevan's – he was Minister for Health – decision that visiting midwives should not carry anaesthetic apparatus. Douglas passed this information on to Bevan who, when he took it in, shouted 'Your wives are nothing but a lot of middle-class hysterics!' Whereupon Douglas responded 'At least they are not childless ones.' Bevan and Jenny Lee, of course, had no children.

In the spring of 1949 Douglas persuaded me, without too much difficulty, not to stand again in the forthcoming LCC election. I had represented Central Hackney for over ten years and left them with great regret. Home claims, however, were increasing and the four-year-old twins needed more, not less of my time. I realize now there were areas of neglect at home which had increasingly upset Douglas, particularly as my work brought in no money. I didn't dust the books and I didn't always have the supper hot and ready, when he managed to get home in time for a meal in the evening. We did, however, on two occasions when the children were babies, manage to snatch holidays away by ourselves, we had our evening walks on the Heath and times of intense shared interest and deep friendship, sitting in front of the coal fire at home.

But the growing demands of Parliamentary and Constituency work for Douglas and the many meetings I was still involved in, despite a short respite from County Hall, meant that we saw less and less of each other as time went on. Sometimes, indeed, we only met on the tube long enough for Douglas to give me the housekeeping money.

Since we both came from a background of generations of unbroken marriages, it hardly occurred to us that the state of marriage itself needed special cultivation.

In June 1949 the Royal Commission Report on Population was presented to Parliament. The panoply and prestige of a Royal Commission were enthralling. The Report starts with the Royal Warrants, presented to King George VI by the Home Secretary, Herbert Morrison. The members are described as 'our truly and well-beloved', and our first chairman, Lord Simon, as 'our right trusty and well-beloved cousin'. The first page of the Report ends with the simple word 'Greeting'. It had a certain prophetic quality and in my view justified Eva Hubback's comments in a review written a few days before her death. She called it 'one of the great State papers of its generation'. Its prophetic quality lay in the recognition that once the birth rate became the result of voluntary decision by individuals, the major limiting factor must be an environmental one. It was the father's occupation that was the deciding factor. Here the Report focussed on the conditions in which mothers actually had their babies. In the Thirties and Forties stillbirths and infant death rates were proportionally far higher in the UK than in any of our West European neighbours. Appointments at clinics and hospitals, the retention of wartime priorities in nutritional policies, the development of family support in crèches and home attendance by doctors and nurses, were all part of our recommendations. The Report found that though the population as a whole enjoyed increasing leisure, the mother of the family remained overburdened and under-recognized. The Commission's view, a wholly original one at that time, was that 'in the process of social advance, until recently the family has been overlooked or given only a minor place in social policy'. The corollary of this being that 'the most important of the non-monetary handicaps of parenthood are felt by mothers who have shared little, if at all, in the growth of leisure in modern times'. That was 1949. In the Seventies my daughter Catherine became a founder member of the Maternity Alliance. She said that the Royal Commission's Report had been a precise description of the aims and objectives of this effective pressure group. Over twenty years on, mothers in many deprived areas of the community still urgently needed to have a fair share of the general rise in the standard of services and opportunities provided.

'The sessions are dull without you' the Secretary of the Royal Commission had written to me while I was away awaiting the birth of the twins. 'There is something in this population problem behind all the things we can label; and I have a feeling that you are the member of the Commission who is most likely to discover what it is.' Could this secret have been my youth and my first-hand current experience of rearing a family? The Commission's researches into mothers' views on the ideal size of a family had revealed the crucial part the third child played in family satisfaction and future population structure. I felt it highly relevant that my own 'marginal child' had turned out to be two!

The introduction of the National Health Service in 1948 was to relieve all income groups (including the better off) of a major financial burden in child rearing. Those of my generation had always assumed that the education service of the future would provide similarly for all sections of the community and set a standard which only the eccentric would wish to buy themselves out of. Douglas and I had always intended that our children and certainly our grandchildren should use and benefit from the national education service. However, when it came to making a choice of school for our children, we had to decide whether their well-being or our principles should come first. In the event, we decided any domestic sacrifice was worth making in order to give all four children the best possible educational start in life. We were only too keenly aware of the advantages of high quality teaching, small classes and general physical amenities which some fee-paying schools could offer. But this did not mean that I in any way slackened my efforts in the battle to improve state education. Quite the contrary. I was ready to see private education abolished. I felt impelled to write a minority note, the first of several, while I sat on the Population Commission, advocating the abolition by law of all fee-paying education and ended the note with the words 'either we must remove the burden of privately financed education from the minds of potential parents in these classes, or we must acquiesce in their failure to replace themselves'. There was, of course, irony in the fact that, unknown to us, the birth rate had climbed steadily during the war – the children became known as the 'post-war bulge' – and was by 1947 the highest recorded since 1920.

When in 1952 I accepted the invitation of North Battersea to become their LCC candidate, I did so with the humorous goodwill of Douglas and the children. On the day the results were announced I was asked to a tea-party for MP's wives at Number Ten. As I was walking along Downing Street, I saw posters announcing that the result was a dead heat. Still breathless from the creaking lift as I arrived at the tea party, I stammered out my concern to Mr Attlee about what would happen next at County Hall. He replied in his calm, clipped tones 'Aldermannic vacancies, aldermannic vacancies'. The constitutional working at County Hall ensured that Labour continued in control by dint of the Aldermannic system and so the dead heat was resolved.

This anecdote vividly illustrates the clarity and sharpness of Attlee's mind. It took other political pundits both at Westminster and at County Hall several days to work out the solution to this apparent impasse.

Attlee was well known for his concise, somewhat minimal phraseology and for his impatience with the irrelevant and garrulous. When the Attlees lived in Essex they frequently had Sunday lunch with their neighbours Judge Crossman, his wife and young son Dick, who was irreverent and turbulent. With his Edwardian background, Attlee clearly felt that children should be seen and not heard, but Dick, fresh from the rigours of intellectual argument at Winchester, knew no such rule. He never stopped tormenting, arguing with and interrupting his father, much to the disapproval of the Attlees. This occasion was so firmly imprinted on Attlee's memory that when, many years later Dick, as an MP insisted on coming to Downing Street, to report on his visit to Israel, Attlee was reluctant to grant the interview. Finally a meeting was arranged but during the whole of Dick's discourse Attlee, pipe in mouth, remained silent. His sole observation at the end of the encounter was 'I saw your mother last week, she seemed very well.'

Once, after a stormy Party meeting at the House of Commons, Douglas was hurrying along the tunnel to the Westminster underground when the Prime Minister appeared at his side. 'Mr Jay,' Attlee proceeded to say, 'I notice you have a hole in your shoe. I have always found a folded postcard excellent for keeping out the damp.'

For fifteen years, Douglas and I worked in the same constituency and they were fruitful years of combined operations. Problems of housing, roads and schools could be pursued jointly through our different fields of responsibility. Our constituents were sometimes confused by our shared name. One lady whom I was canvassing announced 'I have never voted for anyone but Douglas Jay – I never have and I never will – and anyway, why have you got his name?' On being told that I had been married to her MP for several years she replied 'Ah, I see the likeness!' Her vote was secured.

It was a great happiness to me to return to County Hall after a three-year absence. The warmth of my welcome as I dashed up the steps of the main entrance was most marked by the attendants. These kindly and efficient men had occasionally kept an eye on Peter and Martin as they played in an ancient wicker bath chair pushing each other up and down the long corridors at breakneck speed, ending on one occasion with my being called out of the Council Chamber to find that the bath chair and its occupants had landed at the bottom of the marble ceremonial staircase. In spite of a certain amount of gore, both boys were unharmed. Later the same men befriended Helen and Catherine when they came to consume coffee ice-cream topped with golden syrup in the members' restaurant. I became chairman of the Schools Committee and fought many battles for the physical improvement of the Council's schools. The need for this was particularly acute after their wartime use as ARP centres.

Through my work on the Children's Committee which had been set up following the 1948 Children's Act, I became increasingly aware that we were providing an ambulance at the bottom of the cliff rather than a fence at the top. In other words, it was essential that policy should concentrate on the prevention of family breakdown and the support of families under stress. And so a group of us got together and invited Lady Fisher, wife of the then Archbishop of Canterbury, to be our chairman. Together we wrote what proved to be a letter of great significance to *The Times*. We followed this by deputations to the Home Secretary Iain Macleod. He replied 'Your thinking is very near my own.' A chord had been struck and the Fisher group was the inspiration of the chain of events which led to the formation of the Ingleby, and much later, the Seebohm Committees, to look into ways in which social workers could be trained, so as to avoid a multiplicity of visitors for one family. The objective was the prevention of breakdown by supporting families, rather than institutional care following breakdown.

As the financial burden of educating our four children increased, Douglas worked for the *Daily Herald* on Sundays. Peter and Martin were both at Winchester by the early Fifties, and Helen and Catherine moved from the Henrietta Barnett junior school to the North London Collegiate School. We were fortunate in having cheap holidays. The Isle of Wight offered a constant playground of boats and camping; for Douglas's holidays, we kept up the North Cornwall farmhouse lodgings, where to my huge relief, the reluctant housekeeper, the farmer's wife, did the cooking. After breakfast we would collect our sandwiches in small parcels, invariably tied up with darning wool. These, with a bottle of water and a few apples, went into our rucksacks with our swimming gear. We descended to the Strangles by an almost non-existent path from one of the highest cliffs in Cornwall. The beach was so inaccessible that we invariably had the great expanse of sand and rock entirely to ourselves. We swam, played beach cricket, climbed rocks with Peter and Martin, and, by the time they were five or six, with Helen and Catherine. Occasionally, I would just go to sleep in a cave hidden from view. We never had to call on the rescue services, though much later, Peter had to be hauled to safety by coastguards from a cliff face in the West of the Isle of Wight.

Peter left Winchester at Christmas 1954 and in January 1955 came the news that he had gained the Senior History Scholarship at Christchurch, Oxford, and great were our celebrations! There followed two years of National Service in the Navy. He spent most of the time in the Mediterranean as a Midshipman and later as Sub-Lieutenant. As the Suez crisis dawned, letters flew from an anxious father and housemaster to this highly politically aware young man, begging him at all costs to 'obey orders'. These instructions were not really necessary. Martin was Senior

House Prefect at Winchester 1957–8, a position he found fascinating. 'I shall probably never again hold so dictatorial a position' he wrote. In February 1958 we gave a twenty-first birthday party for Peter at All Souls. He was by now an undergraduate at Christchurch, and Martin had arrived at New College. Many children of old friends – Kaldors, Pakenhams and Callaghans were there. Margaret Callaghan, to whom Peter got married three years later, always said she did not remember meeting him on this occasion. The summer of 1960 was a time of treble triumph for Peter. He became President of the Oxford Union, gained a First in PPE and passed top into the Civil Service.

During the Fifties my father's health failed and my parents retired to the Isle of Wight. Their retirement coincided with Peter and Martin's early childhood, so their early memories are of a grandfather who launched boats, chopped wood and lit fires. He continued to adore small children – whoever was the youngest at the table was the focus of his attention. His whole personal life was centred on his family, he hardly had any close personal friends, nor did he find social life in the ordinary accepted sense of the word of interest. As he got older, he concentrated on his immediate growing family circle. When photographs were being taken, he excluded all in-laws, to their great chagrin. Although he seemed to get weaker almost every time I went to visit him, he remained perfectly clear as to my identity and called me his Pegtop to the end. His greatest pleasure, however, was in talking to the children who would bring him their drawings and little presents.

So his death in March 1958 was not unexpected. There was a moving service of thanksgiving for his life in the village church, attended by colleagues from London. Later, permission was given for his ashes to be interred in the floor opposite the altar with an inscription in Greek. I was very touched to have a moving letter of condolence from Philip Noel Baker which perhaps expresses the sort of man my father was better than the more public obituaries. '... A multitude of people remember him with such warm admiration and regard. He had a remarkable talent for making the most important things sound and seem the most important, and of getting all kinds of people, young and old, to work for them with all their power. He played a major, central, indispensable part in making the LNU a great national force – if I hadn't understood then what he accomplished, I should understand it now, for we desperately need someone to do today exactly what he did. And the someone can't be found. It was his brain, his heart, his driving power that made so great a number of his admirers trust and rely on him as their organizer and guide. He was one of the great crusaders for what was, and still remains, the only cause that matters ...' My father's values were an inspiration to my brother John and were later echoed in the work he did for the Industrial Society.

I myself experienced health problems in the late Fifties. These were miraculously sorted out by Jack Piercey of New End Hospital who discovered that I was almost totally devoid of thyroid. My short temper and swings of mood which made home life difficult for all involved, were part and parcel of this deficiency problem. Once set on the course prescribed by Piercey, my health greatly improved.

In 1958 I was asked to become a member of a Government Committee of Enquiry on Human Artificial Insemination. Lord Feversham was the chairman and I was described in the press as 'the commonsense amateur'. My concern was the security and well-being of any child born, whether as a result of insemination with seed of the husband or of a donor.

I was also Vice-Chairman of the LCC 's Welfare Committee by 1958, and increasingly concerned with the problem of London's homeless. One evening in 1961, accompanied by Audrey Harvey, who wrote for the *New Statesman* on housing problems and was a considerable campaigner on homelessness, I visited Newington Lodge.

It was essential that we should appear to be part of the sad queue of women and children seeking admission. Our disguise was not difficult. The scenes that met us have remained indelibly in my mind. There were rows of iron bedsteads, pillows without pillowcases and dark grey, army-style blankets. Meals were served on rough wooden tables while people sat on benches. There appeared to be no nursery provision, little medical advice and above all, no professional social work, involvement, or proper documentation. Was this Elizabethan Poor Law or the mid-twentieth century? Following this visit, there were ferocious battles at County Hall to get changes in legislation. We from County Hall had a deputation to Sir Keith Joseph, Minister of Housing, and we set up a Committee of Enquiry. The background to many of these battles was the unfortunate hostility of people in one class, towards those just below them in the social scale, who had fallen through the net. A forceful lady member, whose husband was a Labour MP in the North East, frequently attacked me, saying her mother had always kept the rent in a teapot on the mantelpiece – why couldn't these homeless people have shown the same careful behaviour? It was strange that I, who had always had a roof over my head and three meals a day, should have identified so much with the awfulness of homelessness. Nor could I fully understand, or sympathize with, the strictures of someone who had suffered far worse deprivations than I ever had.

In December 1962 I saw Hugh Gaitskell for the last time. It was in the Central Lobby of the House of Commons, where at the best of times the lighting makes people look drawn and haggard. I also thought that Hugh, who had recently returned from an official visit to Eastern Europe, somehow suddenly looked much smaller. About three weeks after his return he was struck down by a mysterious illness and spent some time in the Manor House Hospital. He was allowed home for Christmas but he got worse and was admitted to the Middlesex Hospital.

There they diagnosed the virus which had struck him down. But it was too late. He died on 18 January 1963. I cannot improve on Douglas's words in his autobiography. 'Gaitskell's death at this moment was, I believed that night and am even more certain in the retrospect of over fifteen years, not merely an inexpressible tragedy for his friends and the Labour Movement, but a catastrophe for the nation.' Hugh's character was always summed up for me by Matthew Arnold's words 'A will like a dividing spear.'

CHAPTER 7

Tensions

IN APRIL 1964 I was elected to the new GLC for North Battersea with the highest personal Labour vote in the Greater London area. Many of us who watched the old LCC flag coming down felt it was the end of an era. Two members of the family had been closely associated with LCC work: my grandfather William Garnett as secretary to Sidney Webb, and later Education Adviser; and my father-in-law E.A.H. Jay, as Chairman of the Education Committee. The number of boroughs now represented at County Hall had swelled enormously and at the outset the new GLC seemed an unwieldy, impersonal group. I couldn't help thinking of those Outer London boroughs as somehow off the edge of the planet! The personal social services in which I had been so much involved had also disappeared from County Hall.

Two months later, in June 1964, Labour won the General Election and Harold Wilson formed his first administration. The day after the poll was full of nervous tension. Would there be a call from Number Ten to ask Douglas to join the Government? Morning turned into afternoon and still there had been no word. At last the phone rang, it was Downing Street asking Douglas to become President of the Board of Trade. We might have been spared hours of nailbiting uncertainty if Helen and Catherine hadn't been involved in one of their interminable telephone calls on the upstairs extension!

Douglas was immediately transported to the offices of his new department. Later in the day a girl's light voice came through to me on the telephone. 'The President would like to speak to you' the voice said. Thus did Mary Thomas come into our lives. I went to see Douglas in his room at the Board of Trade, cathedral-like in its grandeur, with splendid views over the Abbey and the Houses of Parliament. A slight, slim girl in a simple wool frock brought in a cup of tea. Douglas introduced Mary to me. In these early days of Douglas's time as President of the Board of Trade, my feelings towards Mary were chiefly ones of gratitude. As her job demanded, she was exceptionally efficient in smoothing his working life. Douglas's attitude to her was fatherly and correct. But as their personal relationship grew closer, their whispered conversations in the official car, or playful exchanges at official functions, which I saw reflected in staircase mirrors, made me suffer extremes of aggravation. But even then, I thought of her as one of Douglas's passing fancies. It took me some time to face the fact that Douglas and Mary were growing increasingly close to each other.

Douglas's driver George was also a great pillar of strength and became very dear to us. He had driven Attlee when he was PM. Apparently, once when he was taking Attlee down to Chequers through deep and muddy lanes, they were pursued by the impatient and incessant hooting of a woman driver. In the end, George drew into the side and let her pass. Attlee removed his pipe from between his teeth and said tersely 'Who was that bloody fool?'

'I'm afraid it's your wife, sir.'

'Best say no more about it,' replied Attlee.

George had also taken papers to Churchill at Westerham. The siren-suited figure met him at the front door with the routine question 'Did you come by Hayes Common?' The reply had to be 'Yes sir' whatever route he had taken, as otherwise the great man would have given him a lengthy lecture in the map room on 'the correct route'.

The Labour victory meant for me that the campaign against homelessness could make real progress. I remember urging Dick Crossman, then Minister of Housing, to visit Newington Lodge. He was sceptical when I told him it would be the worst thing he had ever seen. After the visit he told me I was right. We were able to set up a properly run centre for homeless families in London. An old paint factory in Morning Lane, Hackney, was converted. Rooms were created in which families could stay as a group. Play equipment for children, sitting rooms and medical advice were made available. I was particularly pleased when I got it agreed that the Family Planning Association should run clinics at the centre, which meant that many exhausted and distressed mothers were given immediate help without having to travel. It was at the pioneer Morning Lane Centre that professional social workers first won acceptance when dealing with the problems of homeless families. Their involvement had met with great resistance since it was felt there was a high risk of breach of confidence if 'files were left on a bus'.

I was also appointed Chairman of the GLC Parks Committee. The creation and care of open spaces was a cause close to my heart, especially after the loss of the personal social services to the Boroughs. I became especially involved with the development of the 'One O'clock Clubs' in London's Parks, which had already been started by a colleague, Miss Vera Dart. The principal purpose of these groups was to offer young mothers in Tower Block flats a chance to meet each other and to have some break from cramped and isolated living conditions while their children played. They were run on the basic principle of shared care with the staff. Though the midday opening hours of twelve to three excluded working mothers, they fulfilled a great need for mothers with young families who were at home. These groups have become a permanent and much valued part of the London park scene.

The other cause close to my heart was the opening up of the towpaths of London's canals for public use and enjoyment. On a freezing January afternoon, early in 1965, I was taken for a walk by some young friends along the towpath of the Islington Canal behind Noel Road. A scene of desolation greeted us. Old bedsteads and bicycles drifted in the canal while the towpath was locked away from the public behind padlocked gates. I was deeply impressed by the immense loss to public enjoyment this meant. So when I became Chairman of the GLC Parks Committee, I called officials to prepare reports on what could be done to open up the towpaths. I was met with strong opposition from those who said that children would drown in the canal, to which I replied that it was the broken fences, and no-one there to pull children from the water, that caused tragedy. Later, the responsibility for opening and restoring the towpaths fell to the London Boroughs. They each appointed an architect to lay out footpaths, restore and decorate bridges and plant banks with trees and bushes. The whole scheme became part of London's recreational scene and it has proved a great success. This work in the Sixties was the forerunner of many schemes to improve the environment in later decades.

In the early Sixties my son Martin was working for BP in the States and I went to see him in New York, where he was temporarily the proud owner of a tiny flat. He slept on the floor while I writhed in bed in the only bedroom, suffering from oyster poisoning, after a special lunch at the Grand Central Station. The way he looked after me on that occasion was all part and parcel of our closeness to each other. When he returned to England, he acquired his first independent home. It had been a gin warehouse in the Docks, converted into flats by the GLC, with views across the river with all its traffic. I felt a great pang of loss as I sat in my car on the Embankment, after I'd seen him into his new home, though I went on seeing a good deal of him.

Friends sometimes commented adversely on the way I brought up my adolescent daughters. Their ground-floor bedsitting room to which their schoolboy friends had free access seemed to some to exceed the bounds of liberality and to indicate lack of parental oversight. In 1963 Helen and Catherine went to the brand new University of Sussex to read Politics and Sociology. Since their father was President of the Board of Trade, the media took intense and not always welcome interest in the activities of these two long-legged, blonde and beautiful, identical twins. There was an endless stream of press photographs of them in miniskirts. Their sense of fashion caused a minor sensation when they appeared in culottes and toeless white, knee-high boots at a Buckingham Palace Garden Party. Later, they appeared in a coffee-table book called *Birds of Britain*. It was certainly a far cry from what I had been doing at their age and there were some expostulations as to how 'I could let them do it'. But I took pride in allowing them these freedoms. From the earliest years, my daughters and I had felt free to talk with each other. I was confident that all would be well with them. If they had problems they would share them with me and I was able to identify with them. I had myself in my growing-up years often seen adults as authority figures outwitted and even now as a parent I felt emotionally bound to defend my daughters against a (possibly imagined) adverse public opinion. I was also determined that they should not enter the adult world ignorant and unprepared as I had. Later still, when my marriage was falling apart, I was able to share much with Catherine and Helen, too much perhaps, but they gave me sympathy and support. I, for my part, always had the deepest regard for their privacy and growing independence.

In May 1965 I went with Douglas to Amsterdam for the British Trade Week. The highlight of the visit was dining with

Princess Margaret and Lord Snowdon on the Royal Yacht *Britannia*. I sat next to Lord Snowdon and we talked about handicapped children for whom he was seriously concerned. After dinner, Douglas was seated on a sofa next to the Queen of the Netherlands. In a pool of silence fell the Queen's question 'Tell me, Mr Jay, what was the Wolfenden Report about?' This Government enquiry, chaired by Lord Wolfenden, had recently reported on the problems associated with homosexuality, pleading for a more tolerant and sympathetic public attitude. To her eternal credit, Lady Elizabeth Cavendish, then Lady-in-Waiting to Princess Margaret, came quickly to the rescue.

When we got back, some officials from the Private Office met us at Heathrow and drew Douglas aside. He then came over and very gently told me that my mother had died that morning. The news of the death of a parent comes as a great shock, irrespective of one's age. There is a sense of vulnerability, of exposure to fate and a reversion to the dependency of childhood. But for me the overriding feeling at the news of her death was probably one of deep regret that we had not come closer to each other. When I was a young child, she had failed to give me the affection and reassurance I so desperately needed and I suppose I never recovered from that deprivation. Over and above this, came the insoluble problem of her dislike of Douglas. The fierce conflict of loyalties in which this involved me inflicted deep wounds on me. In my confusion I was often impelled to say things Douglas would have approved of when I was with my mother, and vice versa. Also, I could not help feeling hurt that she felt her first grandchildren, our sons Peter and Martin, arrived on the scene before she was ready to play the role of grandmother.

But the holidays my parents had given me and the children in their Isle of Wight house, which I took very much for granted, were a lifeline for me over very many years. My father was still young enough to introduce the boys to canoeing and sailing, and my youngest brother Nicholas, only seven years older than Peter, was a much admired companion in adventures. It was only after my father's death in 1958, however, when I came down to share quiet winter weekends with my mother that I felt I began to know her. We were able to talk of many things. She told me about her intensely happy childhood, the pleasure of ragging about with her brother Ronald and skating on the Cherwell. She told me of the acute disappointment she felt when she found she could not wear any of her trousseau clothes because her first child started immediately after she was married. She shared with me the joy she felt in the new Isle of Wight house where she was able to create a garden and be shielded from the perpetual sight and onslaught of the sea – which she so hated. I came to realize that she was genuinely interested in my personal as well as my work life and looked forward to these weekends with her very much. Though we never touched on her grief over the death of her first-born, I became increasingly aware of the courage it had taken to rebuild her life in the 1920s. All her children remember the total absence of any form of snobbery in her, how she swept aside many aspects of contemporary convention, and above all, her great love of all things beautiful.

Her death had released her from intolerable physical pain. As she lay in her bed in a General Hospital in the Isle of Wight, she had constantly said 'Why does it take so long?' To the eternal credit of my sisters, Pauline and Priscilla, they determined, against medical advice, to bring her home. With her bed in the beautiful sitting room she had created, looking out on to the loved garden, she died within three days of her return. Her funeral, on a glorious May day, was all she would have wanted. The tall grasses studded with buttercups and marguerites were the carpet over which she was carried to the village church. Douglas came to the funeral and held my arm as we said farewell. It pleased me that her many grandchildren's first experience of death should be one of beauty and thanksgiving.

Our first grandchild was born in 1965, the daughter of Peter and Margaret. In a letter to my sister I said 'She has tiny perfect features and enormous dark blue eyes – a face compact with determination and intelligence.' Her names, Tamsin Margaret, gave me great pleasure – the first on account of the Thomas Hardy association, the second because it made a fourth generation Margaret. In the same letter to my sister I commented, with reference to discussion about natural childbirth, that it made me 'feel very old, I just remember demanding the dope quickly'.

Unlike my mother, who had missed her great-grandchild by only three months, I, with a twenty-year gap since the birth of the twins, was wholeheartedly proud, amazed and delighted to be a grandmother. I at once felt a close concern for Tamsin's welfare and happiness and a spontaneous longing to take her to places I had known and loved. It also gave me very great pleasure to share the news about our granddaughter's birth with Audrey Callaghan at County Hall. I took Tamsin to see my aunt Hilda who sang the same songs and played the same games with her that I remembered from my early childhood. Aunt Hilda never changed over the fifty years she meant so much to me. Old Mrs Jay was in her ninetieth year when I took her great-granddaughter to see her. She was frail and breathless but entirely clearminded, strong and determined as ever. She said what a comfort it was to hold a baby on her knee again. Though Peter and Margaret had decided against baptism for their daughter, they accepted a Bible for her in which the great-grandmother wrote words from St John's Gospel.

These words were read at Mrs Jay's funeral, some two months later in December. She died at home after only three days' illness. Her three grandsons and three granddaughters (children of her sons Alan and Douglas) wept unashamedly at the loss of a grandmother of tremendous spiritual and emotional strength who had loved and cared for them all their lives. For me personally her death created a huge emptiness. Gran Jay, as well as loving and caring for my children, had for over twenty years fulfilled the function of an older woman friend. She had the time to give me, and my family, which my own mother did not. She deeply loved and admired Douglas, of course, and it was an enormous relief to me not to have the perpetual conflict of loyalties. I admired and respected her; since she was a reserved person, I really have no idea whether she liked or approved of me. I was, however, often conscious that her extraordinary kindness to me was an indication that she knew that all was not plain sailing within our marriage.

We walked back from her funeral to a changed and lonely Well Road. It was a freezing evening, the stark black branches of trees standing out against the pink sunset of the winter sky.

In August 1966 Douglas and I had been flown from our holiday in Cornwall to Govan's shipyard on the Clyde. The towering sides of the great oil carrier, *British Commodore*, soared over the crowded scene as shipyard workers and local dignitaries cheered her on her slow majestic path down the slipway to the river. Happily, the champagne bottle broke splendidly over the bows as I recited the famous words 'God bless her and all who sail in her.' I was, however, dismayed to see Mary Thomas waiting for us at the airfield and disappointed that the (to me) very expensive pink suit I had had made for the occasion seemed all wrong – the other ladies were all in their dark August Scottish tweeds! Douglas's principle of abstemiousness was under some strain when BP insisted on presenting me with a brooch. Though, on the whole, Douglas was not keen on wives being taken on foreign ministerial visits, I did go to Tokyo with him. There one night I woke to a violent shaking of the bed – an earthquake was in progress. Fortunately, the British Embassy where we were staying had been rebuilt following earlier earthquakes and was reasonably safe. Dinner parties on the Tokyo visit were arranged with a Geisha girl seated between each pair of guests, ready to offer games with matches and so on, if conversation seemed to flag.

Back at home, I remember a party at the High Commission for India, at which representatives of Britain's Labour Government were to meet the Indian Finance Minister. Our unfortunate hostess could not ask her guests to go in to dinner as George Brown, the most senior British Minister, had not arrived. After nearly an hour, he rushed in without particular apology. I found myself at a small circular table sitting next to him. Still ruffled, he suddenly glared at the Governor of the Bank of England and in front of the Indian Finance Minister exclaimed 'The trouble with all of you is that you simply don't try!' Hardly the impression our hosts wished to give to their guest of honour!

Though there was as yet no question of divorce, our marriage was showing signs of strain. Each felt that the other could no longer give the affection, companionship and appreciation each so desperately needed. When I tried to talk to Douglas, he was unresponsive. 'I must read, I must read,' he would say, leaving me feeling pretty suicidal. On such occasions when we needed a refuge and a friendly word of advice we both sought out Shiela, separately, of course. After one such occasion, she wrote 'It is really pathetic, his great need of you. I was amused the way so much of each of your visits to me is taken up with endless talk about each other. I really think it is a great tribute to the depths of your feelings for each other and in a cold unfeeling world you both shine out. It is very remarkable among all the couples one meets, utterly bored with each other after only a few years of marriage, how you each crave so much more of the other and are both so certain that the other one has it to give if only they will. I don't think I have ever realized before how much Douglas needs you to help him and look after him nor what intense possibilities still exist in your relations with each other.' Those words were oil on troubled waters, for a little while at least.

1967 was a year of personal disaster for both Douglas and

me. In April of that year, I lost my GLC seat, and in September, Douglas was asked to leave the Government. I lost my seat owing to the existing electoral procedure though I again had the highest personal Labour vote in the whole GLC area. Candidates had to fight for their seats in teams of three or four on a borough-wide basis. The new London Borough of Wandsworth consisted of two parliamentary seats held by Conservatives, one marginally held by Labour, and one, North Battersea, my own, solidly held by Labour. This situation, at a time when public feeling was running against Labour, resulted in my defeat. After almost thirty years on the LCC and GLC, the whispered message that I had lost in the cold hours of dawn in the Town Hall came like the clang of doom. I don't know how I should have sustained this loss without the personal support of my undergraduate niece, Virginia Garnett, daughter of my brother, John. For days we had canvassed together, climbing tower blocks and talking on draughty street corners. However, her appetite for politics was whetted and later, as Virginia Bottomley, she was elected to Parliament, becoming Conservative MP for Mid-Surrey after Maurice Macmillan's untimely death. She is now Minister of State at the Department of Health.

After taking Virginia home to Putney, I drove back to Hampstead. I remember standing at the bedroom window at 4.00 am as dawn broke over London. Douglas woke up and, though sympathetic, did not appear surprised. 'I thought it would be so,' he said. His response seemed cool but it was in fact the distanced statement of world-weary politicians of long standing 'bloodied but unbowed' who can survive the blows and buffets of outrageous political fortune. But, in my heart-breaking unhappiness at this moment, I did rather long for something more comforting.

I got this, as so often, from my brother John, who wrote 'What a bitter, bitter blow! But my dear wonderful girl, I know you won't let it crush you and that somehow you will get your strength – as we get it from our parents and from each other – to give courage to the people who helped you . . . all I know is that out of failure comes the greatest move forward and achievement.'

In September, Douglas and I were on holiday in Postbridge, our long loved Dartmoor hide-out. One evening a telephone call came from Harold Wilson in the Scilly Isles. He asked Douglas to meet him at midnight in the station master's office in Plymouth. As we drove across the moor, the dark night was studded by the reflections of our car lights in the eyes of the grazing sheep. We drove along with a sense of foreboding. Since the Government's inception in 1964, Douglas had been out of sympathy with many in the Cabinet on the issue of the Common Market. True to his deeply felt antagonism to Britain's membership of the EEC, he had worked at every level for a review of Government attitudes and a halt to current trends. He never trimmed his sails or sacrificed his principles. When he emerged from the interview, white and shaken, I knew the blow had fallen – the Prime Minister had sacked him on the Common Market issue. Touchingly, the first thing that Douglas told me was that the PM had said that now Douglas was no longer a Cabinet Minister, he would like to do something about a life peerage for Peggy, 'a useful woman'.

As we drove back across the moor, I fancied my sympathy and concern were of some comfort to Douglas. But already his true source of strength and comfort lay elsewhere. The following evening, the hotel telephone rang and Douglas leapt up to answer it. Mary Thomas had kept her promise to leave the Civil Service, where she had a very bright future, in order to work privately for Douglas. She came to Dartmoor the next day to help him answer the flood of kind and supportive letters which arrived by every post. I returned home to pick up the pieces of public and private shipwreck.

Even now I did not perceive Mary Thomas as a threat to

my marriage – nor in any conscious deliberate way was she. She was caught in the crossfire of the disintegration of a longstanding, deeply felt relationship between two sad and angry people. By this time I felt quite unable to help Douglas so that when Mary came to rescue Douglas on Dartmoor while I went back home, I felt grateful to her. As I did when she came on Sunday evenings, to our Chiltern cottage, to keep Douglas company. We had rented this cottage from Mountbatten's son-in-law, David Hicks. I had embarked on setting it up and furnishing it with great enthusiasm as a new start in our marriage. But as time went on, I realized that nothing had really changed.

There were enormous pressures to keep the marriage together though the recent deaths of both our mothers had somewhat relaxed these pressures and may, indeed, have precipitated the crisis. But longstanding family traditions of lifelong marriages, and above all the wish not to upset out grown-up children, still held us together. Nor was I myself ready to contemplate life without Douglas. I finally found the strength to do this through the help of a remarkable psychotherapist, Ingrid van der Post. She was in fact the last student trained by Jung himself in Zürich. She would say to me on my weekly visits to her in her penthouse behind Chelsea Town Hall 'I am not interested in whether or not you get divorced, nor where your next meal may come from. We are here to talk of far more fundamental issues than that.' The whole process of clarification and healing was mysterious and one for which I was wholly grateful. She was a warm, accessible person through whom I learnt much about myself and who made me feel that in spite of all difficulties there was much in life to look forward to. 'My dear, self-awareness is a bitterly painful process' she wrote to me in July 1968. 'As the defences come down and life pours through it carries away so much with it. But it also waters the ground for new growth. Please believe this – and particularly you who have so much life stored up inside.' At the end of two and a half years I said 'I think this is the last time I shall come to you.' 'Yes', said Mrs van der Post, 'I felt it would be so.'

Helen and Catherine had recently left Sussex University and joined the job-hunting, flat-seeking young in London. Both found jobs in television: Helen with ITV, Catherine with the BBC, and both found flats in Notting Hill Gate where they enjoyed an ever-widening social life. I think it was a relief to them to leave the tensions of home life behind them. They had both been amazingly sympathetic and supportive to me through these later disturbed years.

The loss of the GLC seat had meant the end of a way of life. For almost thirty years County Hall had been my place of work. The office, work with Council officials, debates in the Council Chamber and in Committees, private meetings and deputations from the public had made life an immensely absorbing challenge. And I should be less than honest if I failed to say how much the personal friendships with other members and lunchtime conversations in the members' dining room had meant to me. Among the older generation of colleagues I remember the quiet dignity of Lady Nathan, the frightening clarity of mind and sharp political acumen of Margaret Cole, the compassionate and original ideas of Vera Dart and the solid work of Helen Bentwich, with whom I frequently clashed on the Education Committee.

Of my own contemporaries most dazzling was Bea Serota, later Baroness Serota. She arrived at County Hall after the war from the Hampstead Borough Council where her youth, beauty and intelligence had made her the toast of the town. She was recognized as a first-class administrator and immediately promoted to the Whip's office, later to be the first Chairman of the Children's Committee. Tact, courtesy and charm were her weapons and the walls of Jericho went down before them. Marjorie McIntosh (Barbara Castle's sister) was another remarkable woman. She combined bringing up a family, lecturing at Bedford College with being Chairman of the Education Committee. This often involved as many as three separate school functions a day – in different parts of London. The Council in those days provided no transport for her. I remember returning in our car from a constituency meeting in Battersea and seeing her standing at the bus stop on the dark, wet street. She was wearing a long evening dress and carrying a bouquet. We stopped and took her home. A few months later she died from a stroke, cut off in her forties as a direct result of overwork and lack of support. Needless to say, all future chairmen of the ILEA were provided with an official car. Audrey Callaghan was a close friend and became closer as we shared grandchildren. Her quiet, friendly, commonsensical manner achieved many things. Later, when Bea Serota was Minister of Health, Audrey was appointed Chairman of Great Ormond Street Hospital, where her experience as a member of the LCC Children's Committee was invaluable.

My salvation came from four new pieces of work which now offered themselves. In the summer of 1967, Kenneth Robinson, then Minister of Health, asked me to join the North West Metropolitan Regional Hospital Board. In 1968 Dick Crossman asked me to become Chairman of Friern Psychiatric Hospital Management Committee. Later, I was asked to join the Parole Board. But perhaps the most abiding interest for the next twenty years was the Heath and Old Hampstead Society of which I became Chairman in 1968.

CHAPTER · 8

The Health Service and the Bench

IT WAS at a tea party in the damp, rather sunless garden of Number Ten Downing Street that I found myself talking to my friend, Kenneth Robinson. The Chairman of the North West Metropolitan Regional Hospital Board was Sir Maurice Hackett, brother-in-law of George Brown. He was indefatigable and, according to one's point of view, intransigent and somewhat aggressive. We were soon locked in controversy. All that I had learnt twenty years before at County Hall about child care seemed to be wholly ignored. There was no form of family or group care, no continuity of staffing in the care of mentally handicapped children. Some wards had thirty changes of staff in a month, nor was there adequate parental contact. There was no physio or other form of therapy. There were simply rows of crying children, either lying on the floor, or tied in chairs round the wall. From this date in 1968 I determined I would never abandon the cause of getting these children out of the long-stay hospital system.

I persuaded the Board to vote a sum of money which would convert the children's wards into small group units with greatly improved play opportunities. Though this was done, the change had not, alas, taken root in the hearts and minds of the staff. Visiting Harperbury some ten years later, as Chairman of the

North Camden Community Health Council, I found toys stacked on the balconies and children seated in lines waiting for their dinner to arrive. The report we made on this situation so angered the COHSE Branch at the hospital that they wrote to Barbara Castle, then Secretary of State for Health, demanding my removal from the Chairmanship of the Committee of Enquiry into staff training, for the care of the mentally handicapped, which she had asked me to undertake. Happily, she ignored the request.

The next point of conflict with the Regional Board was over my appointment as Chairman of Friern Psychiatric Hospital. I had received a call from Dick Crossman to come to his room at the DHSS. I met him and Bea Serota, who was Minister of Health, and without further ceremony Dick said, 'I want a damned great explosion in that place, but for God's sake make it a controlled one.' This request followed much press publicity on the report 'Sans Everything'. The late Sixties saw the beginning of public anxiety about long-stay Psychiatric and Mental Handicap Hospitals. My appointment to Friern was the tip of the iceberg. Sir Maurice Hackett's reaction to my appointment was to ask for my resignation from the Regional Board. As Secretary of State, Dick Crossman told Hackett he could choose between resigning himself or keeping me on. He decided to keep me.

My first thought was to improve conditions for the staff. My experience of residential work at the LCC had taught me it was essential to care for the carers. The improvement of staff houses and setting up a staff coffee bar were among the first things I did. Then, with the advice of a professional interior decorator, I saw to it that the wards were made pleasant, though this upgrading by no means met with universal approval. 'You can get used to anything' was one sister's reaction. I was very proud indeed, however, when at the end of five years, Friern Hospital was judged the best long-stay hospital in the Region by the Hospital

Advisory Service. The local Member of Parliament was (and is) Margaret Thatcher. She regularly attended hospital occasions and had an infallible memory for detail. 'Shall I write to Mr Crossman?' she would say, gazing at a piece of worn-out linoleum not replaced since her last visit. She was also genuinely concerned for the welfare of the patients, making a point of seeking out the sickest person, and the most junior members of staff. She did not stand on ceremony but sat with the workers, professional and voluntary. At this stage, of course, Mrs Thatcher was an opposition MP who had appeared as a busy and effective person. On a more personal level, however, I was amused by her confiding in me that when her twin son and daughter had returned that day from their respective schools, she had been most anxious for them 'to learn how the other half lives and not grow up with any sense of privilege. So I asked them to go and sweep out our swimming pool,' she said.

I was invited to join the Parole Board very early in its existence, and the work there was most exhilarating. The gentle wisdom and authority of our Chairman, Sir John Hunt of Everest fame, made a fine counterpoint to the sharp minds and sparkling wit of the judges. The experience and compassion of Probation Officers sometimes contrasted sharply with the idiosyncratic dicta of the psychiatric members. When the case of an arsonist came up for Parole, the psychiatrists differed violently on the degree of risk involved in releasing such a man. In a case of incest (which had been closely studied in the family setting) the psychiatrist who had been against the arsonist urged release for the man serving a sentence for incest. His colleague, (there were always two psychiatrists present) urged precisely the opposite in both cases. Not unnaturally, lay members found all this somewhat confusing.

I had been appointed to be a Justice of the Peace in 1964 and served on the Bench for the next twenty years, earlier having been on the London Juvenile Bench. This involved travelling all over London for weekly attendances over a three month period. The Juvenile Court JPs were an impressive bunch, more especially their Chairmen. I did sometimes ask myself whether a court of law was the right setting for trying to solve tragic family situations which were responsible for the child's appearance in court. On other occasions, I was disappointed that years of effort by social workers had not really resulted in any improvement with the family and child. But the Court provided a forum in which various points of view could be aired and the Court's power to reach a decision, frequently came as a relief to all concerned.

For many years I served on the adult court in Hampstead. I realized with some dismay, that some members of the Bench had absolutely no idea what it was like to live on a weekly income. Since I lived on a low income myself, I was acutely aware of issues like rent and rate rebates. For instance, a fine of fifty pounds to a single parent running a black and white TV without a licence would be catastrophic, leaving no money for shoes for the children to go to school. On the other hand, a fine of fifty pounds to a motorist was often hardly felt. I used to urge a more realistic understanding of the accused's actual financial position.

In the mid-Sixties, our old friend, Sir Christopher Cox, invited me to be his first woman guest at the New College Feast of St Thomas. It was one of the first occasions on which women were allowed at the 'High Table'. The first course for those of us at the High Table was oysters. As the roar of conversation from those in the Hall who were not feasting on oysters enveloped us, we at the High Table began to display signs of acute discomfort. My symptoms were chiefly visual as my surroundings seemed to disappear down a long dark tunnel. I was by no means the first to leave the table in confusion. There followed a night of horror: it was freezing January and the only bathroom available to the guest room was through a labyrinth of passages and quads exposed to the icy night air. I never ate oysters again.

In January 1969 our younger son, Martin, married Sandra Williams. They had known each other at Oxford but she had done much travelling in Brazil since those times. Her father was Chairman of ICI at Welwyn Garden City and they had a huge wedding reception at the ICI Welwyn offices. As is perhaps inevitable when a mother has had a particularly close relationship with her son Sandra and I took a little while to warm to each other. But the path with Sandra soon became smoother as we understood each other better and I was entirely behind her in the immensely difficult task of establishing a balance between getting her medical training and bringing up their three children Claudia, Tabby and Adam. She knew how much I approved of what she was trying to do, and she succeeded, not least because Martin took such a willing, open-hearted part in the child rearing. He would take them away for weekends to their Exmoor cottage while she was working for exams or doing her hospital stint.

In April of the same year, I visited Peter who was *Times* Correspondent in Washington. He and Margaret were living in a very pretty house in Georgetown, with red squirrels nesting in the garden. I visited them in time to celebrate the first birthday of their second daughter, Alice. While I was there, I visited Mrs Dean Acheson, who intrigued me by enthusing over the joys of breakfast television. Rather poignantly she said that for a woman who had travelled the world on great occasions of state with her husband, keeping up with breakfast time news filled a considerable vacuum in her life. This was some years before Peter became involved with the setting up of TV AM at home.

Before coming back to England I visited Catherine, who was camp-following with a student whom she had met at Sussex University and who was now a Kennedy scholar at Harvard. The congestion in their tiny flat in Cambridge, Massachusetts, was intense. I remember sleeping in a kind of cupboard into which their conversation drifted through the long hours of the night.

My personal life was drawing nearer disaster. The relationship between Douglas and myself deteriorated to such an extent that we did not talk to each other any more. On my return home from Washington I switched planes at Dulles airport, hoping that I would in this way avoid being met by anyone. So I was astonished to have Mary Thomas visit me almost as soon as I got home. As always, being an optimistic and credulous character, I was persuaded that all was well and that I should try yet again to restore the marriage. Twelve months later, the ghastly procedure for the break-up of the marriage was set in motion.

It was during this painful period when the marriage was definitely breaking up, that I decided, on three separate occasions, to break away from my monogamous way of life. I found the affairs flattering and amusing but the emotional strain of such relationships and the sense of guilt and confusion they caused me meant that they ended almost as soon as they had begun – with a sigh of relief on my part.

By the end of the Sixties Douglas and Mary Thomas were sharing every aspect of their personal and working lives. As far as I was concerned, it was losing him as a partner in work that was most painful, though it would certainly be true to say that the passionate aspect of our marriage survived until virtually the end of the road. I had known since before we were married that Douglas had no intention of being technically faithful to me. He was no hypocrite in these matters though I confess I was not prepared for all that was in store – all those ladies with Douglas's hand on their knees! I had reached a point at which I could no longer tolerate the sharing of my personal life with Mary Thomas. The children were grown-up and launched and I was determined now that Douglas and I must part. I know when the final break-up came, both daughters only wished it had come sooner. My sons were shocked and deeply regretful.

It was no easy decision. After forty years I still thought of marriage in terms of a great romantic, passionate dream. For forty years I had, as it were, sat at Douglas's feet, learning nearly all I knew from him, constantly fascinated by his agile mind and sparkling conversation. In spite of everything, I admired him. An intense shared interest in politics, our children and the family holidays had made a strong enough bond between us to sustain the marriage. But Mary Thomas had moved progressively nearer to our Hampstead home – from Fulham to Primrose Hill to Frognal. During the 1969 General Election campaign, they canvassed together, were closeted in the Party office together, ate together. I was left out in the cold. When the poll was declared, the other candidates thanked their wives for their help and support. There was no word for me from Douglas. From his point of view, I suppose, it was my emotional outbursts, though understandable in many ways, that he found most unbearable and particularly distasteful. Since childhood he had been disciplined never to give unbridled reign to his emotions. Moreover, he held the considered view that 'he could never understand the meaning of the word forgiveness'. Many are the occasions on which I had banged my head against this insurmountable wall of intransigence.

As my children grew up, I was fascinated to observe the profoundly liberating and soothing effect created in marriage by the financial independence of wives. My own total financial dependence on Douglas was a relic of Victorian–Edwardian days. It was also partly my own fault. I had never conceived of doing anything but voluntary work, which was not even eligible for attendance allowances. Money, or rather the lack of it, was the flash point of many disputes between Douglas and myself.

I realized, too, that for may years, indeed, until his mother died in 1965, I had played a 'daughter' role in relation to Douglas. After his mother's death he seemed to expect me to switch to being a mother figure. This I could not and would not do. As I approached the age of sixty, I felt deep stirrings of independence. Where my work was concerned, I had led an integrated and adult life for many years. My personal life, however, was still one of domestic servitude, due largely to the fact that Douglas had to come up with the money for everything. Perhaps it was this factor above all others that finally proved fatal to the marriage.

As far as I was concerned then, the time for talking, for all those heartbreaking discussions about compromises that were never made, was over. My impression was that what Douglas would really have liked was for me to continue in the Well Road house, providing continuity for the children and, at some very basic level, for himself. But I was no longer prepared to do this. I was greatly strengthened in my determination to make the break, by my psychotherapy sessions with Ingrid van der Post. Once the matter was in the hands of our respective solicitors – in Douglas's case Theodore Goddard who had dealt with Mrs Simpson's divorce – there was no going back. We were all determined to avoid press publicity, so the division of possessions was quietly settled, the children between them persuaded Douglas to agree to a financial settlement for me and there was nothing left for the court to decide. My last sight of Douglas was of him walking down the staircase in Well Road carrying his large and ancient Jaeger dressing gown.

Then came the divorce itself. I remember the nightmare sensation of standing in the witness box at the Law Courts as the Judge asked if the marriage had broken down irrevocably. Forty years, reaching back to my schoolgirl days, were about to be declared null and void. 'To my very great regret – yes,' I heard myself say from dry lips.

When I got back to my daughter Catherine's house, her husband, Stewart, handed me a letter from Douglas. 'Darling,' it began and went on with a list of a number of the positive aspects of our marriage, more particularly emphasizing his pride in our four children. He could not, however, forego even this last opportunity of reminding me of the ways he felt I had failed in my obligations as his wife. 'You must surely understand how deeply before anything I am attached to continuity and loyalty and constancy ...' Constancy from me, of course, rather than from himself. '... things would have been different if you could just have understood simply that I meant what I said.' I don't suppose he realized the enormity of that 'just'. As I read his letter, I was overcome with immeasurable weariness. For the last time I had been offered a stone where I had hoped for bread. It was not until 1972, in the last letter I had from him, on the anniversary of Peter's operation that he said he was probably to blame for much though he wished I could have understood him better.

One great joy lit up the dark days of my crumbling marriage. On a Sunday morning in August 1970 on the Isle of Wight, my brother John, walking back across the fields from church, told me that he had decided to divide the family home at Horestone Point into two flats. He asked me if I would like to use the small inheritance I had from my mother, to buy a ten-year lease on the upper flat. The offer came at exactly the right moment for me, the conversion work was put in hand and the setting up of the flat absorbed my waking hours. My parents' bedroom, with views to the sea, became the sitting room, their bathroom became the kitchen and the huge dormitory at the top of the house was split into two large double bedrooms and a single bedroom. The old box room, with a new window, became a grandchildren's bunk bedroom. For ten halcyon years, children, a growing number of grandchildren and friends, enjoyed this new holiday home with me. At the crack of sunny dawn, long before their parents were stirring, I would give breakfast to two or three benappied infants. As we made expeditions to the Table Rock and the House Rock, I rediscovered the magic of the rocks and pools of my own childhood. Later, I introduced the children to the delights of very small boat life, rather pleased to find that my own sense of balance and other seagoing expertise had in no way deserted me. Quite often, my two sisters, Pauline and Priscilla, as well as my brother, John, would have their children and grandchildren there.

The rocky promontory of Horestone Point divides the beach into two distant bays. My brother and sisters and I spent many happy hours 'visiting' each other in our respective bays, arriving at our destinations either with a procession of elderly prams, or in small boats, with a trail of small people carrying buckets and spades. During the Easter holidays a fourth generation was enjoying beach hockey, in the same place where my parents had first met, some seventy or eighty years before. The sound of John chopping wood in the garden during these holidays or his car approaching in the lane always gave me a great lift of spirit, just as the sight of the chained doors of his boathouse signified the end of the holidays and meant a sinking of spirits.

In January 1970 our daughter Catherine married a young barrister, Stewart Boyd, whom she had met through his sister who was a colleague at the BBC. Though Douglas and I were scarcely on speaking terms by this time, this marriage was a great happiness to both of us. Like Douglas, Stewart had been to Winchester. Like him also, he was totally committed to hard work and personal integrity, and was passionate about sailing and gardening. The actual wedding was something of an ordeal since my imminent divorce from Douglas had become widely known and nobody felt that family photographs were the order of the day. I like to think we surmounted our personal difficulties well enough to give the pair a good send-off, in the Crypt Chapel of the House of Commons, and at the reception in one of the great rooms opening off the terrace of the House of Commons. Indeed, such was the throng of friends and relations that there were complaints of overcrowding. I resolved at this wedding, as I had at Martin's that I would make every effort to build friendship on firm foundations with my children's marriage partners. In no way did I want to see the failure in relations between my husband and my mother repeated. There was so much about Stewart's background and way of life that we could share that I have always felt totally at home in his house. He and Catherine started married life in Wimbledon. After the birth of their first child, Rachel, they moved to Kentish Town and then, to my great joy, they arrived in Hampstead to live in the house which had belonged to John le Carré while he was writing *Smiley's People* – only five minutes walk from my home in Well Road.

I had decided to sell the small remaining lease of our house at 12 Well Road, where we had lived since 1944. I moved into the flat in the semi-basement, for to continue to live in this familiar spot was one of the healing aspects of life after the break-up of the marriage. My sunny bedsitting room, overlooking the quince tree in the garden has given me lasting pleasure, though it is strange to look out of the window onto the house where I grew up and where my brothers and sisters were born. Strange, too, to live next to the house where I first saw Douglas in the garden he loved.

So my new life began in 1972 and I was instantly enchanted with it. The relative absence of domestic chores meant a delightful addition to the time I could spend doing things of deep personal interest and satisfaction. In my reading, I turned to biography with increasing pleasure. Reading about other people's lives, whether from the distant or recent past, helped me to emerge from my very sheltered background and to identify and sympathize with the aims and aspirations of my daughters and daughters-in-law. I also discovered the dark green, beautifully produced Virago paperbacks which introduced me to many women writers I had never come across before and led me back to some old friends like Rosamond Lehmann, Vera Brittain,

Winifred Holtby and Elizabeth Bowen. Reimmersion in past and present thinking on the position of women helped me, as had my sessions with Ingrid van der Post, to resolve some of the deep-rooted contradictions on my evaluation of myself as a woman. My father had been firmly convinced that men were superior beings, an attitude reinforced by his mother who felt that women were there to provide the creature comforts that men were supposed to require, including larger quantities and superior quality food. I must have absorbed this attitude through the pores of my skin, for I remember being teased by my daughters and daughters-in-law for making just such assumptions.

When my mother and sisters hobnobbed about 'women's topics' such as dressmaking and cooking, I longed to be involved with them. At the same time, I also wanted to be apart, if not superior, to all that. On my mother's side of the family there was a long tradition of university educated women and certainly neither at school at St Paul's nor at college at Somerville, did I ever doubt my equal status with men. Now for the first time in my life, I was neither daughter, wife nor mother. I was alone. I was myself.

The days were so busy and strenuous with work in central London, the evenings restful and enjoyable in front of my television. To choose my own programme and watch it without interruption was absolute bliss. I could sit and knit while watching the box and supplied the growing number of grandchildren with simple sweaters, which constituted the limit of my knitting skill. I gave the occasional supper party for old and new Hampstead friends, but soon found that I could entertain with less effort and most enjoyably in the little restaurant at Burgh House.

Just as I was finding a new equilibrium, came the most agonizing night of my life. Over Whitsun 1972 I was on my way to the Isle of Wight on the Friday when a fierce storm blew up and all car ferries were cancelled. To the sound of a roaring gale and crashing waves, I spent the night in a Portsmouth car park, listening to the angry waves and the mewing of my cat to her new-born kittens as I thought of Douglas about to be married to Mary Thomas. Gradually, dark turned into dawn, Saturday passed and on Sunday, there, in the papers, were the photographs of Douglas with his new bride.

They had bought a cottage in Hampstead Grove and unhappily, from my point of view, I frequently met them in Hampstead High Street. We did not acknowledge each other, nor indeed at the many children's and grandchildren's social occasions which we both attended. To my great relief, they moved to the Cotswolds after a few years and I was spared these awkward encounters.

In 1975 our daughter Helen got married to David Kennard, a young BBC producer. I was much charmed by his good looks though I did not feel I knew him at all well. There was none of that instinctive feeling or familiarity which I had with Stewart. They, too, got married in the Crypt Chapel of the House of Commons. The toast to the bride and groom was moved by Robin Day of the BBC, followed by a fascinating speech from Professor Kenneth Galbraith with whom David was working at that time on the series *The Age of Uncertainty*. Alisdair Clayre, a friend of David's and author of the novel *The Window* also spoke. Helen and David's first home was in Barnes. David was used to a free and easy lifestyle, always on the move, travelling all over the world. Domestic life, with the addition of two little girls by the end of the Seventies, did not fit in with this *modus vivendi* and the marriage broke down. To their credit, Helen and David have remained great friends.

The Seventies saw a great change in my work life, too. Community Health Councils were set up and I became Chairman of the North Camden group. Our task was to try and reflect public needs and views on the Health Service. For this purpose, I insisted that we needed to work closely with the Health Service

Management groups. We were fortunate that the first, and succeeding, Chairmen of Camden and Islington Area Health Authority not only welcomed CHC representation at their meetings but gave me, as their representative, generous opportunity to put forward the concerns of those who lived in North Camden. In these early days, the CHC Chairmen often led the discussion. Our grassroots knowledge enabled us to dispute official reports and to raise new issues.

The relationship with our other management group, the Royal Free Hospital, was not quite so warm. As Chairman of the Heath and Old Hampstead Society, I had for many years opposed the Royal Free moving from Gray's Inn Road to Hampstead. We argued their plans would cause gross over-development of the Pond Street site and increase an already acute traffic problem; both points have, in fact, been abundantly proved true. This meant that, as far as the Royal Free was concerned, I was not the most popular person. Indeed, Dame Frances Gardner, powerful Dean of the Medical School, had eyed me with suspicion for some years as we both sat on the Regional Board. But, of course, the Community Health Council's relationship with the great new teaching hospital was more fundamental than a clash of personalities. For almost a century the Royal Free Hospital had provided a service of great value to the crowded working class area round King's Cross. As its founder had intended, the hospital gave invaluable help to the multitude of social and medical problems created by three great railway termini.

I constantly urged the senior doctors and administrators to try to understand that the transfer to Hampstead would mean serving a very different kind of community, which had used University College Hospital when it needed the skills of a great teaching hospital. It was an uphill task, but little by little relations improved, a process which was greatly helped by the arrival of the new Dean of the Medical School, Dr MacGillivray.

In 1975 Barbara Castle, Secretary of State for Social Services, set up a Committee of Enquiry into training of staff who worked with the mentally handicapped and I was asked to become the Committee's Chairman.

I found this deeply satisfying in many ways. After many years of slogging it out in the field, I had been given the opportunity to draw together the many threads of work for the mentally handicapped, particularly that relating to children. The work would, I hoped, prove to be 'a milestone in the care of the mentally handicapped'. As well as the National Health Service nurses, our terms of reference included Residential Care Workers from the local authorities. In the introduction to the Report we made three years later, I said that the appointment of the committee had been seen 'as a logical and inevitable reflection of mounting public concern about the quality of life of mentally handicapped adults and children in residential care. A major aspect of this concern has been the conditions in which some mental handicap nurses are working.' The Committee was made up of some eighteen members. They were a joy to work with, friendships grew and were greatly valued, and unanimity was maintained until the last weeks of the existence of the Committee. I particularly remember Mr Hunt, the Director of Social Services in Hampshire; Derek Thomas, a young clinical psychologist from Northumberland, who is now director of the Hospital Advisory Service; Mrs Betty Nicholas who, as education officer of the General Nursing Council, proved most constructive and helpful. I also remember Dr Derek Ricks who, as a result of my own efforts when I was on the Regional Health Authority, had, as a consultant in charge of the children's department at Harperbury Hospital, virtually cleared up the children's wards and instituted a system of outreach and community care. His sad, early death was an irreplaceable loss to this work.

Perhaps my greatest gratitude was to the Civil Servants who assisted us. Liz Woods, then an Assistant Secretary at the DHSS had superlative drafting skills. At a residential weekend held by the Committee I decreed we could not go to lunch until a certain paragraph of the draft report had been agreed. When no agreement seemed to be forthcoming, Liz Woods offered to try her hand, while we revived our flagging energies. She had a new draft ready when we got back on which there was instant agreement. Our Secretary was Denis Dufton. His humour, tact and concentrated work survived even our most Spartan visits. One was to Northumberland in a freezing February. We were accommodated in an old Italian prisoner-of-war camp, where the bedrooms contained one pillow, one blanket and a Bible.

When our report came out, urging that staff should be trained to work either in NHS or Local Authority Residential Care, and that the number employed should be doubled, Barbara Castle was said to have remarked 'If I hadn't expected a controversial report, I would not have appointed Peggy Jay.'

The *Nursing Mirror* campaigned against the Report. Later, many nurses said that if they had understood what the Report was actually urging they would have supported it. But as it was, nurses in uniform would meet us carrying banners with the slogans NO WAY MRS JAY and WE'LL HAVE OUR SAY. The *Nursing Mirror* campaign had, wholly unjustifiably, whipped up fear in the nursing profession that our Report was recommending a loss of status and even jobs. In fact, the reverse was true. We recommended a doubling of the workforce caring for the mentally handicapped, and a huge expansion of responsibility and opportunity both for nurses and residential care workers. In the end, there is no doubt that the Jay Report did prove to be a milestone in the development of training for those working with the mentally handicapped. Both the Royal College of Nursing and the social work trainers have had several joint working parties and there is a good deal of shared training now for those who come in to work in the nursing profession and those who come in as care assistants through local authority social work service. Another of Barbara Castle's courageous initiatives was to form the National Development Group which met as a quango in the DHSS, under the Chairmanship of Professor Peter Mittler. I was determined to make an all-out effort to close the children's wards for mentally handicapped children in the long-stay hospitals and offer alternative and improved forms of care. In the Seventies there was still resistance from the medical profession to this line of thought; there was much threatening talk from doctors on the National Development Group about the 'health needs' of these children.

When the Group was abolished, I decided to set up another called Exodus. We were supported by major voluntary organizations in the field of mental handicap, including MENCAP and the Spastics Society. The latter gave us great encouragement and on-going help. Our purpose was simply to see the last child out of the long-stay hospitals and now professionals do recognize that no child should be in a long-stay hospital. Their number has been drastically reduced but if those remaining are not to spend the rest of their days in hospital, the Government has got to find the money for local community services. Responsibility for these services should be moved from the National Health Service to the local authority, with the necessary medical support and oversight.

One of the most enjoyable and worthwhile pieces of work throughout the Seventies was my Chairmanship of the Heath and Old Hampstead Society. It was founded in 1897 to preserve the Heath in its natural beauty and to ensure that its managers, the London County Council, did not create a park-like appearance with neat edges, hard paths and bedded out geraniums. The Bill Sir John Gurney Hoare MP introduced into Parliament in 1871, marked the birth of the Heath as we know it. In the 1930s Lord Ilford, better known as Geoffrey Hutchinson, fought to prevent high-rise buildings going up round the edges of the Heath and a kind of spaghetti junction of motorways intruding onto the Heath. The Heath Society has co-operated closely with the GLC and its staff and this has been the secret of the Society's effectiveness. During the 1970s the Society risked a major split on a point of principle. Owing to the absence of grazing animals, the open grassland on the Heath was becoming steadily lost. As seedlings turned into thickets and thickets into small woods, neither grass nor flowers grew for lack of sunlight. Half of the Heath, which I had known as open grassland fifty years ago, had become impenetrable thicket and the potentially explosive issue was how best to maintain the natural wild beauty of the Heath with the minimum of human intervention. Some thought not a leaf or branch should be removed, but I said that in that case we would lose the Heath. I was fortunate to recruit to the Society's Committee several highly dedicated young enthusiasts of the Heath who, in cooperation with the Heath staff, saw that a certain amount of human intervention was needed if the openness, of what is essentially heathland, was to be preserved for future generations.

CHAPTER · 9

Hampstead: Contentment Regained

ONE EVENING in the spring of 1977 Peter rang up and said that he had some news for me and would be arriving about midnight. As we sat over coffee he talked about the Washington Embassy. I had no clue where this conversation was leading, when suddenly he came out with the fact that he had been appointed UK Ambassador. It was overwhelmingly exciting, but I was sufficiently politically aware to realize that all hell might well break loose with charges of nepotism, since Peter was the Prime Minister's son-in-law. It is a tribute to James Callaghan's courage and integrity that he accepted David Owen's recommendation of Peter for the job since he, better than anyone, knew from where the cold wind might blow. In the event, the great majority of letters to the papers on the subject came down firmly in favour of Peter's appointment as Ambassador.

I felt a great sense of occasion when I visited Peter and Margaret in May 1978. Margaret met me at Dulles airport, with two members of the Embassy staff, who swept me through the customs. As we drove into Washington, I had my first experience of a car telephone with a welcoming call from Peter. Although I had visited the British Embassy when John Freeman was Ambassador, I had never actually stayed there. In fact, the Embassy, designed by Lutyens, with its rose brick and steep pitched roof was keenly reminiscent of Hampstead Garden Suburb, also designed by him. The garden, indeed the whole city, seemed afloat on magnolia, dogwood and cherry blossom. My immediate impression was how skilfully the stately home on the ground floor had been combined with the family home on the first floor, reached by a spiral staircase. I was in a corner suite complete with sitting room and bathroom, which had recently been occupied by Mrs Thatcher and Princess Margaret.

It was a time of hopefulness and achievement for Peter and Margaret. Washington took this young and handsome British couple to its heart and they, in their turn, took their duties seriously. Margaret was an accomplished hostess and imbued official occasions with a sense of personal welcome and pleasure. Often the great ballroom with its tall blue lapis lazuli pillars was given an air of informality by substituting round tables, at which people could talk over dinner, for the more formal narrow ones. Margaret also had many speaking engagements all over the States, particularly on the subject of the National Health Service in Britain. The Americans were amazed at the efficiency of the NHS and could hardly belive that what you got free at the point of need could be as good as what you paid for.

Peter and Margaret's children Tamsin, nine, Alice, seven and Patrick, four, were thriving on a happy mixture of the American lifestyle with its hot-dog, sleep-over birthday parties and the ordered English nursery life with nanny in charge. President Carter's daughter Amy, ten, shared some classes with Alice. On one occasion Amy came to take part in a performance of *Midsummer Night's Dream* in the ballroom. When the performance was over, the children enjoyed sliding over the polished floor in their socks. Almost immediately Amy got a splinter in her foot and was escorted upstairs by Alice's nanny, closely followed by two enormous uniformed guards, whose holsters were clearly visible under their jackets. These faithful henchmen never let her out of their sight, leaning against the bathroom door as the splinter was removed, murmuring that they didn't think they would have much trouble there.

One of the highlights of my visit was a Gala spring concert in New York celebrating the life and work of Benjamin Britten who had just died, with Dame Janet Baker and Peter Pears singing in Britten's Spring Symphony.

Two years later I returned to Washington in less auspicious circumstances. Peter's appointment as Ambassador had inevitably ended on Mrs Thatcher's electoral victory in 1979. Contrary to Foreign Office tradition, Peter and Margaret stayed on in Washington, where Margaret had a job with one of the US Television Networks. Then, back at home, Peter presented Channel 4 *Week in Politics* for three years from 1983 as well as editing the monthly *Banking World*. He also continued as Chairman of The National Council of Voluntary Organizations for five years. In 1986 he returned to his first love, administration, as Chief of Staff in Robert Maxwell's publishing empire – where he is at present.

Towards the end of the Seventies I became involved with the setting up of Burgh House in Hampstead with the Chairman of our Trust, David Sullivan, and our Curators Christopher and Diana Wade. Together we embarked on the exciting and deeply satisfying task of providing a centre and focus for the myriad activities of Hampstead village. For me personally, the little restaurant in the basement provided a meeting place for the renewal of many old friendships.

The first group were people with whom I had been to school, and of these, Pat Plowright is the one with whom I got back into closest touch. Then there were people with whom I had pushed prams in the Forties and Fifties, the Fairfax Jones's, the Massinghams and the Stephen Wilsons. We enjoyed remembering our childrens' parties, the Christmas holiday games of hockey which I had organized on the Heath on Joad's hockey ground, named after C. E. M. Joad of the Brains Trust. For almost thirty years I had been so involved with work in central London that these associations had been allowed to lapse. To renew them at the end of the Seventies was the greatest possible pleasure.

It was at Burgh House that my four children gave me a memorable seventieth birthday party in January 1983. It was the last time we six brothers and sisters were to be together. Within the next two years, Michael and Priscilla had died. But on 28 January we were all in celebratory mood. The grandchildren, all eleven of them, were the focus of much liveliness and fun. My eldest granddaughter, Tamsin, made a speech which was a triumph of gentle irony. Her reminder that her grandmother insisted only red and blue clothes should be worn on the Isle of Wight holidays caused much laughter, both among adults, who had had to provide those clothes, and the children, who had been subjected to this particular obsession of mine. When I spoke, I threaded my thoughts on Thomas Hardy's poem *Heredity*.

I am the family face;
Flesh perishes, I live on,
Projecting trait and trace
Through time to times anon
Leaping from place to place
Over oblivion.

The years-heired feature that can
In curve and voice and eye
Despise the human span
Of durance – that is I;
The eternal thing in man
That heeds no call to die.

The grandchildren were a living demonstration of what Hardy was saying in that poem. Martin rounded off the speeches by saying what an inspirational Mama I had been and such loving words, even if undeserved, were, of course, most heartwarming.

Almost all the parents of my children's husbands and wives were there, which gave me particular pleasure. As always, James and Audrey Callaghan brought their own particular warmth without the least touch of grandness.

My longstanding friend, Baroness Serota, spoke of our County Hall days and some of the audience were startled to hear her say that I had been the 'Red Ken' of County Hall in the Fifties and Sixties, terrifying many senior members with my ferocious radicalism. Shiela Grant Duff spoke of a friendship lasting almost sixty years from the time we were twelve-year-old schoolgirls to the decade when we entered our seventies. There were Hampstead friends going back to my childhood and the early days of my marriage like Stephen and Patsy Wilson, Pat Plowright and Tessa Fairfax Jones, as well as more recent friends acquired during the work on the Burgh House venture like David and Ann Sullivan, Ed and Brit Wolf, Christopher and Diana Wade, Barney and Margaret Rodgers.

It was round about this time that I finally decided the time had come for me to leave the Labour Party, after half a century or so of loyal and active membership. It was the unmitigated horror of the Hampstead Labour Party General Committee meetings which proved to be the breaking point for me. For years I had known of their disaffection and remember voting in a minority of one when in the Fifties they were demanding Hugh Gaitskell's resignation as Leader. I recall a sense of almost physical fear as the bully boys of the Far Left, with their naked class hatred and Marxist dogma, poured out their violent animosity. I knew that the public would not respond to this. These people were a colossal electoral liability who would make it impossible that there should ever again be a government to the Left of Centre.

Above all it was the dangerous doctrine of unilateral disarmament constantly being peddled which drove me out of the Labour Party. Having spent my childhood and youth with my father championing the cause of collective security and multilateral disarmament, I felt that the cry of 'peace in our time' was prostituted on the lips of these Labour Party members, as indeed was the word 'democracy'. Nothing has threatened the independence of Members of Parliament (and therefore of Parliament itself) more than the principle of reselection which necessitates a constant and regular review by the local general management committee for the sitting MP. A member who wants to make a constructive and uninterrupted contribution to his constituency is constantly undermined, as he or she awaits the next caucus meeting of activists, wondering whether his position will be confirmed. The whole fabric of response to local needs is wrecked by a system which puts power into the hands of a small minority of political activists who are rejected by the electorate at polling time.

After many years of stress I found the Social Democratic Party under the leadership of 'The Gang of Four' (Roy Jenkins, Shirley Williams, David Owen and Bill Rodgers) a true political haven. I had known them all over the years. Shirley Williams had, like me, been to St Paul's and Somerville, albeit at a later date. I had always admired her common sense and capacity to grasp the main point of an argument. Never more so, indeed when, as a member of the Parole Board, I would occasionally meet her as a Junior Minister at the Home Office. I had known David Owen, chiefly as Minister of Health, and greatly admired his drive and determination. I knew Bill Rodgers in various local government capacities and thought highly of his abilities. My perception of Roy Jenkins was somewhat misted through Douglas's intense disapproval of the whole Common Market issue, but I knew him to be a man of great breadth and experience. Besides, Douglas and Roy's political differences did not prevent Roy being a guest at our table in Hampstead, nor Douglas and me from playing tennis with him in Notting Hill.

In the Eighties I became a member of the Liberal Democrats

and my regard for the leader of this Party, Paddy Ashdown, has continued to grow.

However, my party political work receded as my concerns for Hampstead grew. I think the work I have done as Chairman of the Heath and Old Hampstead Society – twenty years in 1988 – has been the most worthwhile and satisfying in my life. Hampstead, with its crooked roofscapes, its village lanes and narrow byways, the breeze blowing fresh across the Heath, has indeed been my homestead and the backdrop to the vicissitudes of my life. When I became Chairman in 1968 I had close and recent links with the management of the Heath which were an advantage to the Society. I had been Chairman of the GLC Arts and Recreation Committee, 1964–7, when I lost my North Battersea seat. So the tradition of working in close cooperation with the Heath's managers initiated by previous chairmen, in particular Lord Ilford, continued. My immediate predecessor, Lord Cottesloe, now our President, had contributed his invaluable negotiating skills.

In the dialogue between the Society's members and the Heath staff, the need for tree control is increasingly recognized, so that the Heath will not have turned into an impenetrable thicket in fifty years' time. The Heath is, of course, also under constant threat from would-be developers who have their eye on every nook and cranny, garage or garden on its borders. The Society is determined to prevent what has happened in many Royal Parks round which high buildings have sprung up, ruining the sense of open country which is one of the splendours of Hampstead Heath.

I myself am constantly involved in major and minor battles. The telephone in my little Well Road flat rings at all hours. I have been known to fly out in my dressing gown at the crack of dawn to try and prevent trees being felled without due authorization. Sometimes I fight a losing battle in this area – notes of authorization are held under my nose, and even as I make last desperate phone calls I hear the noise of electric saws doing their dastardly worst. Sometimes the outcome is more positive: someone rings to say a historic pillar box is about to be removed. 'Tie yourself to it', I say and even if my words are not taken absolutely literally, militancy saves the day. Not for nothing has the London Standard called me the erstwhile Boadicea of County Hall!

Between public commitments I fit in a rushed visit to the hairdresser in Flask Walk, 'Kiki', where I never fail to meet a kindred spirit. Once I found myself sitting next to Michael Foot. I wailed to him about the dark political age we are living through, saying that the introduction of the Poll Tax would be a reversion to Tudor times. 'Plantagenets you mean, Richard II' came the unhesitating reply.

Our local paper, the incomparable 'Ham and High' is the very essence of Hampstead. With its political and arts pages of national standing, it is read far beyond the boundaries of Hampstead and Highgate. The secret of its success lies in the gifted personality of its editor, Gerald Isaaman. While maintaining the highest standards, he has made the paper a stunning commercial success, for he has the knack of keeping the cooperation even of those whom he attacks. Estate agents, for instance, whose unsightly boards are the subject of constant protests, are induced to contribute generous sums to the Heath Society!

These last fifteen years on my own have been a time of fulfilment and happiness. People ask me if I am lonely. My answer is that the relationships which are so necessary to me, with my brothers and sisters, my sons and daughters, my grandchildren, and friends old and new, flourish on the fertile soil of solitude.

Until recently my sister Pauline lived near Pangbourne. Here, as in her Isle of Wight cottage, she created a sense of welcome and concern for all. Never did anyone keep her lifelong friendships in such excellent repair. Postcards arrived marking one's comings and goings, anniversaries were remembered, indeed

Pauline had become the family archive. Sometimes we reversed our roles of older and younger sister – she alone remained who might criticize the length of my petticoat or lack of polish on what burglers have left of my silver. It was this sense of personal caring which made her such a life-enhancing person. She died in August 1989 after a short illness. After her death, the warm centre of extended family life had gone and the hearth was cold.

Since my brother John retired as Director of the Industrial Society, he has been appointed Chairman of the West Lambeth Health Authority, based at St Thomas's Hospital. Here he does battle with the extreme left-wing Lambeth ex-councillors who bring neither constructive thought nor sympathetic concern to the NHS officials battling with the financial crises of the Health Service. By coincidence, John's first wife, Barbara, is engaged on the other side of Westminster Bridge at County Hall, doing similar battle on similar problems. She is a senior professional teacher and was elected as a Conservative member of ILEA in 1984. As a hard-working member of the minority party she undoubtedly finds the Extreme Left complexion of many of the Labour members a threat to the education service.

My younger brother, Nicholas, is a comprehensive school master in Oxfordshire. His wife, Jean, organizes education for children with special needs in Coventry. They, like Pauline and John, are proud owners of a holiday cottage on the Isle of Wight. It is here that family contact and continuity is maintained for all of us. We introduce new grandchildren with special pride and joy and watch them grow to love the island. From buckets and spades, to helming in junior sailing races, it is all there, and provides a living thread of continuity for the oldest generation. There is a certain corner of Seagrove Bay, the site of my grandparents' house where I spent many childhood months during the First World War, where the sweep of the bay and the small rocky headland with the trees behind it, fill me with an aesthetic and spiritual exhilaration that is quite extraordinary.

Peter got married for the second time in January 1986 to Emma Thornton. They had met sailing in West Cork. After Cambridge, Emma taught history and then joined the ILEA inspectorate, advising secondary schools on the teaching of history. Later, she turned to designing garden furniture. They live in the Victorian family house in Ealing which has been Peter's base for nearly twenty years. Their son, Thomas, born in 1987 is a cheerful character with his mother's brilliant blue Scandinavian eyes. He now has a brother, Samuel, born in 1988.

Martin and his wife Sandra have left Islington and now live south of Winchester where they have bought a lovely house. From this base Sandra works as a GP and Martin sets forth as a Divisional Director of GEC. He has continued as a pillar of helpfulness throughout my life. It is pleasing to see this quality reappearing in his nephew Matthew, Catherine's son. Like Martin, Matthew has the gift of defusing a family crisis with a well-timed joke.

Helen married Rupert Pennant Rea, editor of the *Economist*, in June 1986. She and her two young daughters Amanda and Juliet, joined forces with him and his children, Rory and Emily, in an extended house on the edge of Wandsworth Common, where Helen and Rupert's son, Edward, was born. Helen has found the domestic challenge she had always sought: a husband with a demanding job, several children and a spacious house.

Inevitably, I see most of Catherine who lives just round the corner from me. In January 1985 she and her husband Stewart bought Wraxall Manor, a grey stone Jacobean house of great beauty folded in the green hills of West Dorset. Catherine had taken me with her on a freezing, snow-covered day on a house-hunting expedition. From the moment she saw it, she knew this house was what she and Stewart had been looking for. They have made the house a base for family and friends and have become an integral part of the local community.

In August 1987 Catherine had a little daughter, Hannah.

Before the birth of this child, she worked for the Spastics Society and wrote a book on the prevention of handicap called *The British Way of Birth*, which was part of the Society's 'Save a Baby' Campaign. Catherine's closeness to me, in all senses of the word, is a major source of happiness to me. I share her concern for the children, she in her turn makes me feel cared for. In sickness and in health, in success and setbacks, in our shared friends and conversations – political, social or personal – Catherine has made a warmhearted centre to my life.

In March 1987 I was invited to Douglas's eightieth birthday party, though he still felt unable to speak to me. It was held at Peter's house in Ealing and I met Bryan Gould there for the first time. He made me feel nostalgic for the Labour Party of the immediate post-war period, for he seemed to me to be a man of intelligence and integrity in the Attlee–Gaitskell mould. I also met Maire Lynd and Clarissa Kaldor again, who had been my seniors at St Paul's. As we three elderly ladies sat in a quaint row on three upright chairs, I was made aware that our long established friendship was overlaid with political differences of a rather fundamental nature – as always on the issue of unilateral disarmament. I sometimes meet Maire who has, like me, lived in Hampstead all her life, flyposting for causes from which I keenly dissociate myself!

In October 1987 Douglas was elevated to the House of Lords. He comes up to London two days each week from Minster Lovell in Gloucestershire where he and Mary now live.

In January 1988 I celebrated my seventy-fifth birthday – I have now reached the stage in my life where the calendar is punctuated at frequent intervals by birthdays of special significance within the circle of the family and friends. The party came as a total surprise. En route for what was to be a small dinner party at my daughter Catherine's house, we stopped to call in at Burgh House, ostensibly for a message. I opened the front door to a room crowded with all the people I love best, family and friends, singing Happy Birthday. David Sullivan, Chairman of the Burgh House Trust, in speaking of my work for the Heath made much of the importance of the element of myth and legend in private and public life. My brother John, conjured up images of boyhood teas in my room at Somerville with great warmth and enthusiasm. Odd remarks overheard stay in the mind. 'Douglas Jay is such a clever man', from my sister's husband Roland Hunt; and his son Julian, a fellow of Trinity College, Cambridge, recalling the fact that Aunt Peggy made sure he knew all about the birds and the bees! The Callaghans were there to hear our granddaughter Tamsin announce her engagement to Simon Raikes making it a double celebration and adding an invigorating note of family continuity. Following their marriage in September 1989, they have come to live in a flat in my daughter Catherine's house, thus making the fifth generation of my family to take root in Hampstead. Indeed, a good many of the fifteen grandchildren were present, including the youngest, Hannah.

For me the evening was joyful and fulfilling. After fifteen years of silence, Douglas spoke to me. He and Mary gave me a pot of lovely blue hyacinths and Douglas made some casual remark about not forgetting to water them.

About a year after this I retired from the Chair of the Heath and Old Hampstead Society, although I continued my work for the Heath, as I had been asked to represent the Society on the Heath Management Committee of the Corporation of the City of London. My final Annual General Meeting at Burgh House was presided over by Gerald Isaaman, Editor of the *Hampstead and Highgate Express*, whose loyal support of the Society, as indeed of all Hampstead causes, has been of the greatest possible value. The occasion was a happy one for me – all my four children were there as I took my formal leave with a bouquet of flowers from the new Chairman of the Society.

So now I have just over three quarters of a century behind me. Walking on the shadow of my life, the past lengthens, the future is foreshortened. In spite of all the difficulties, in spite of anger and some bitterness, Douglas has been the touchstone of my life. It was he who sharpened my intellect and opened up the world of politics to me. Together we had children. In them and their children the threads of our lives are inextricably interwoven.

The passage of time imposes huge changes in one's role as parent. Moving from the driving seat to the backseat, I have tried, not always successfully, to avoid the pitfalls of backseat driving. Happiness comes now in watching the children achieve fulfilment in their personal and professional lives.

As far as my own personal fulfilment is concerned, after years of disapproval from parents and husband, it is only during the last nineteen years when I have been alone, that I have discovered a self that I can like and approve. My childhood problems gave me the driving force for a life's work. My relationship with Douglas showed me how this work might be achieved. Out of pain my own creativity has grown. My greatest vindication has been the confident optimism with which our children have felt it worthwhile to build homes and families of their own.

Index

Acheson, Alice (Mrs Dean), 113
Adam, Ruth, 69, 79
Age of Uncertainty, The (Galbraith), 121
Ahmed Mirza, Shah of Persia, 11
Alfriston, 48
All Quiet on the Western Front (Remarque), 43
Amsterdam, 98–9
Ann Veronica (Wells), 22
Arnold, Matthew, 19, 93
Asquith, Herbert Henry, 6, 11
Attlee, Clement (later Earl), 7, 86–7, 95
Attlee, Violet (later Countess), 77, 95

Baker, Dame Janet, 129
Balogh, Thomas (later Baron), 47
Banking World, 129
Bazely, Sir Thomas, 46, 48
Beaconsfield, 66
Bembridge (I.o.W.), 17, 24
Bentwich, Helen, 107
Betjeman, Sir John, 24
Bevan, Aneurin, 47, 83
Bevin, Ernest, 56
Binyon, Laurence, 20
Binyon, Nicolette, 20
Birds of Britain, 98
Bottomley, Virginia (niece), 82, 104
Bowen, Elizabeth, 120
Bowlby, Dr John, 19
Boyd, Catherine (daughter) – *see* Jay, Catherine
Boyd, Emily (granddaughter), 75, 81
Boyd, Hannah (grandaughter), 136, 138
Boyd, Matthew (grandson), 136
Boyd, Rachel (granddaughter), 119
Boyd, Stewart (son-in-law), 116, 118–19, 121, 136
British Union Of Fascists, 57
British Way of Birth, The (Boyd), 137
Brittain, Vera, 43, 119
Britten, Benjamin, 129
Brontë, Emily, 75
Brooke, Rupert, 8
Brown, George (later Lord George-Brown), 103, 109
Burford, 48

Callaghan, Audrey (now Lady), 101, 108, 131, 138
Callaghan, James (now Lord), 127, 131, 138
Cambridge (Mass.), 113
Carter, Alice, 128
Castle, Barbara, 122, 124
Cavendish, Lady Elizabeth, 99
Cecil of Chelwood, Robert, Viscount, 12, 23
Change and Fortune (Jay), 60, 78, 93
Chatham, 51
Children and the Law (Garnett), 8

Index

Churchill, Randolph, 43
Churchill, Sir Winston, 95
City of London School, 11
Clayre, Alisdair, 121
Cohen, Helen, 79
Cole, Margaret, 107
Common Market, 105, 132
Community Health Councils, 121–2
Constable, John, 13, 59
Cottesloe, John Fremantle, Lord, 133
Council for Education in World Citizenship, 64
Cox, Sir Christopher, 39, 42, 67, 112
Crackington Haven, 81
Crossman, Erica, 35
Crossman, Helen, 87
Crossman, Richard, 35–6, 37, 83, 87, 96; at DHSS, 108, 110, 111
Crossman, Judge Stafford, 87
Crowther, Geoffrey (later Baron), 47, 79, 132
Crowther, Margaret (later Lady), 79, 132

Daily Herald, 56, 89
Dalton, Hugh (later Baron), 49, 56, 70
Dalton, Ruth (later Lady), 49
Dart, Vera, 96, 107
Davenport, Nicholas, 48
David Lloyd George's War Memoirs, 74
Day, Robin (now Sir), 121
Duff, Shiela Grant, 41, 45; as school friend, 20–21, 131; as confidante, 30–31, 32, 34, 53, 55, 69, 80, 103; relationship with Douglas, 31, 32, 33, 37, 38, 53; and women's place in society, 80
Dufton, Denis, 124
Durbin, Evan, 81–2
Durbin, Geoffrey, 79
Durbin, Marjorie, 82
Dusty Answer (Lehmann), 21

Economist, 47, 136
Edinburgh, Prince Philip, Duke of, 74
Education, Ministry of, 6
Edward VII, 19
Exodus group, 125

Fairfax Jones, Tessa, 131
Falkender, Marcia, Lady, 78
Family Planning Association, 96
Feversham, Charles Duncombe, 3rd Earl, 91
Fisher of Lambeth, Lady, 88
Floud, Peter, 33–4
Foot, Michael, 134
Franks, Oliver (now Lord), 67
Freeman, John, 127
Friern Psychiatric Hospital, 108, 110–11
Fry, Roger, 46

Gaitskell, Hugh, 47, 51, 59, 82, 83, 131; illness and death, 92–3
Gaitskell, Dora (later Baroness), 47, 59
Galbraith, Professor Kenneth, 121
Gardner, Dame Frances, 122
Garnett, Barbara (sister-in-law), 82, 135
Garnett, Christopher (nephew), 82
Garnett, Hilda (aunt), 2, 101
Garnett (now Hunt), Hilda Rebecca Pauline (sister), 16, 75, 100, 118; birth, 10; marriage, 66; in India, 66, 69; close relationship with, 134–5
Garnett, Jan Nicholas Palmer (brother), 45, 55, 69, 79, 100; birth, 28; career, 135
Garnett, Jean (sister-in-law), 135
Garnett, John William Poulton Maxwell (brother), 41, 44, 138; birth, 14; rapport with, 15, 82–3, 104, 118; war service, 69; and Industrial Society, 83, 91; family home in Isle of Wight, 117, 118, 135; later career, 135
Garnett, Kenneth (uncle), 9
Garnett, Margaret (*née* Poulton) (mother), 21, 40, 64; first meeting with future husband, 1, 118; birth of children, 1, 10, 12, 14, 23, 28; appearance and character, 3, 17, 100; loss of first son, 4, 54, 100; miscarriages and illness, 4, 5, 6; ancestry, 4–5; loss of brother and sisters, 6–8, 9–10; life at

Hampstead, 13–14, 15, 16, 17; conflict with Peggy, 17, 22, 99; and Isle of Wight house, 24–5, 82, 90, 99, 100, 117; strained relations with Douglas, 33, 37, 38, 39, 42, 45, 53, 99, 119; and birth of grandchildren, 53, 74; Oxford home, 59, 79; wartime community kitchen, 48; purchase of Hampstead house, 70; death, 99–100, 101, 106
Garnett, Maxwell (father), 18, 20, 99, 120; first meeting with future wife, 1, 118; character, 3, 9, 64, 90–91; happy marriage, 3–4, 64; idealistic and educational work, 3, 6, 11, 63–5; loss of first son, 4; loss of brothers on war service, 8–9; growing family, 10, 12, 14, 23, 28; background, 11, 13; as General Secretary of League of Nations Union, 12, 15–16, 63–4; financial problems, 16; strained relations with Douglas, 33, 37, 38, 42, 45; Oxford home, 59, 79; forced resignation from LNU, 64; retirement and death, 90–91, 100
Garnett, Michael Ronald (brother): birth, 12; war service, 69; death, 130
Garnett, Peter (brother), 1, 18, 54; death, 4, 100
Garnett, Priscilla Janet Cecil (sister), 69, 100, 118; birth, 23; death, 130
Garnett, Sybil (aunt), 9
Garnett, Stuart (uncle), 8–9
Garnett (now Bottomley), Virginia (niece), 82, 104
Garnett, Dr William (grandfather), 11–12, 23, 94
Garnett, Mrs William (grandmother), 49, 120
General Elections: (1935), 51; (1945), 77; (1964), 94; (1969), 115
George VI, 83, 84
Goddard, Theodore, 116
Goodbye to All That (Graves), 21, 43
Gould, Bryan, 137
Govan, 102
Graves, Robert, 21, 43
Gray, Miss (St Paul's Girls' School), 19
Greater London Council (GLC), 107; Arts and Recreation Committee, 133; Labour Party, 94, 104; North Battersea, 94, 104, 133; Parks Committee, 96–7
Greenwood, Anthony (later Baron), 41, 43
Guest, Haden, 49

Hackett, Sir Maurice, 109, 110
Hailsham, Quintin Hogg, Lord, 36
Hampstead, 12, 13–17, 29–30, 53, 68, 77, 112, 121–2; Babies' Club, 54; Burgh House, 129–31, 137–8; 'Chestnuts, The', 9, 13; Foley Avenue, 13–16; Frognal, 50–51, 54; Frognal School, 14, 17; Heath and Old Hampstead Society, 108, 122, 125–6, 133–4, 138; Labour Party, 131; Well Road, 70–71, 119, 133; Well Walk, 13, 30, 45, 59, 67
Hampstead and Highgate Express, 134, 138
Hardy, Thomas, 28, 46, 101, 130
Harperbury Hospital, 110, 123
Hart, Professor Herbert, 40, 62, 67
Hart, Jennifer, 40, 67
Harvey, Audrey, 91
Hathrop Castle, 48
Henderson, Sir Hubert, 72
Heredity (Hardy), 130
Hicks, David, 106
Higgins, Twistington, 59–60
Hill, Oliver, 24
Hinton Manor, 48
Hoare, Sir John Gurney, 125
Holst, Gustav, 19
Holtby, Winifred, 120
Hopkinson, David, 69
Hubback, Camilla, 40
Hubback, David, 40
Hubback (later Hopkinson), Diana, 20–21, 31, 41, 69
Hubback, Eva, 11, 20, 72, 73, 84
Human Artificial Insemination, Committee of Enquiry on, 91

Index

Hunt, Sir John (now Baron), 111
Hunt, Julian (nephew), 138
Hunt, Pauline – *see* Garnett, Hilda Rebecca Pauline
Hunt, Roland (brother-in-law), 66, 134, 138
Huntley, Thomas, 5
Huntley and Palmer, 5, 24
Huxley, T. H., 22

Ilford, Geoffrey Hutchinson, Lord, 125, 133
Industrial Society, 83, 135
Inside Number Ten (Falkender), 78
Isaaman, Gerald, 134, 138

Jay, Adam (grandson), 113
Jay, Alan (brother-in-law), 39, 70, 74, 101
Jay, Alice (granddaughter), 113, 128
Jay (now Boyd), Catherine (daughter), 40, 78, 94; birth, 74–5; early years, 79, 81, 88, 89; and Maternity Alliance, 85; education, 89, 98; employment, 107; in America, 113; marriage, 118–19; closeness to, 136–7
Jay, Claudia (granddaughter), 113
Jay, Douglas (now Lord), 14, 63, 81, 86; first contacts with, 26, 27–8, 119; encourages Peggy in studies, 28, 29–30, 34; journalism, 29, 30, 47, 56, 89; elected to All Souls, 29, 31; growing friendship with, 29–38; considers monogamy a sin, 32, 51, 114; strained relations with Garnett parents, 33, 37, 38, 39, 42, 45, 53, 99, 119; engagement, 35; flirtations and affairs, 37, 39, 51, 55, 95, 102, 114–15; unconventional views, 38, 42, 55–6; marriage, 45–6; political and social circle, 47–8, 49, 50–51, 132; attitude to children, 52, 53, 62, 73, 75, 80, 117; as *Daily Herald* City Editor, 56; and son's illness, 60; incipient strain on marriage, 61, 83–4; war years, 63, 66–7, 70–71, 76; at Ministry of Supply, 67, 71; as economic adviser to Attlee, 77–8; as MP, 78, 87; at Board of Trade, 94–5, 98, 102; increasing strain on marraige, 103, 105–6, 114–16, 118; leaves Government, 104, 105; divorce, 116–17; second marriage, 121; eightieth birthday, 137; elevated to Lords, 127; and Peggy's seventy-fifth birthday, 138
Jay, Edward Aubrey Hastings (father-in-law), 39, 48, 49, 63, 66, 71, 94
Jay, Emma (daughter-in-law), 136
Jay (now Rea), Helen (daughter), 78, 94; birth, 74–5; early years, 79, 88; education, 89, 98; employment, 107; marriage, 121; second marriage, 136
Jay, Helen (sister-in-law), 27, 28, 39, 75; death, 29
Jay, Isabel (mother-in-law), 27, 39, 47, 48, 51, 55, 63; closeness to grandchildren, 54, 60, 66, 71, 74, 101; death, 101–2, 106, 115
Jay, Margaret (daughter-in-law), 90, 101, 113, 127–8, 129
Jay, Martin (son), 48, 63, 130, 136; birth, 61, 62; early years, 65–6, 68, 70, 71, 74, 78, 80, 88, 90; and birth of sisters, 75; education, 89–90; at Oxford, 90; in America, 97; marriage, 113, 119
Jay, Mary (sister-in-law), 27, 39, 48, 63, 66
Jay, Patrick (grandson), 128
Jay, Peggy (Margaret Garnett): birth, 1; childhood, 1–4, 5–6, 9, 10–12, 13–26; family background, 4–5, 11–12; family holidays, 11–12, 23–6, 27–8, 135; schooldays, 17–22; conflict with and distance from mother, 17, 22, 29, 38, 99; unhappiness and insecurity, 18–19; early friendships, 20–22, 30, 131; first contacts with Douglas, 26, 27–8, 119; study for Oxford entrance exam, 27, 29–30, 34; growing involvement with Douglas, 29–38; coming-out dance, 31; at Oxford, 34–44;

engagement, 35; university friends, 35–7, 40–41; growing political awareness, 42–4, 49–50, 51; joins Labour Party, 43, 44, 49, 50; marriage, 45–6; domestic inefficiency, 46–7, 49; social life, 47–8; and problems of poor families, 49–50, 56; reforming zeal, 50; distress at Douglas's infidelities, 51, 55, 95, 114–15; birth of children, 52–4, 59, 61, 62, 72, 73–5; emotional outbursts, 55, 115; election to LCC, 56–8; and children's illnesses, 59–60, 81; strains on marriage, 61, 84, 103, 105–6, 114–16, 118; war years, 63, 65–76; constituency work, 68, 87; on Population Commission, 72, 73, 85, 86; neglect of home duties, 83–4; leaves LCC, 83; and state education, 86; rejoins LCC, 86, 87–8, 91; marriages of children, 90, 113, 118–19, 121, 136; death of father, 90–91; health problems, 91; and problem of London's homeless, 91–2, 96; election to new GLC, 94; and care of open spaces and towpaths, 96–7; visits to America, 97, 113, 127–9; relationship with daughters, 98, 136–7; death of mother, 99–100; grandchildren, 101, 117–18, 120, 130, 135, 136; loses GLC seat, 104, 107, 109; psychotherapy, 106, 116; and Health Service, 108, 109–11, 121–5; local activities, 108, 125–6, 129, 133–4, 138; on Parole Board, 111; as JP, 111–12; break-up of marriage, 114–16; fleeting affairs, 114; divorce, 116–17; holiday home, 117–18; new independent life, 119–21, 134, 137–9; and care of mentally handicapped, 123–5; seventieth birthday, 130–1; leaves Labour Party, 131–2; flourishing family relationships, 134–7; seventy-fifth birthday, 137–8
Jay, Peter (son), 48, 101; birth, 52–4; early years, 54, 55, 57, 65–6, 68, 70, 71, 74, 8, 90; serious illness, 59–60, 117; and birth of sisters, 75; education, 79, 89–90; National Service, 89; at Oxford, 90; marriage, 90; in America, 113, 127–9; as UK Ambassador, 127–9; later career, 129, 136; second marriage, 136
Jay, Sandra (daughter-in-law), 113, 136
Jay, Tabby (granddaughter), 113
Jay, Tamsin Margaret (granddaughter), 101, 128, 130, 138
Jay, Thomas (grandson), 136
Jenkins, Roy (now Lord), 132
Joad, C. E. M., 129
Johnson, Celia, 20
Joseph, Sir Keith (now Lord), 92
Journey's End (Sherriff), 43
Juliana, Queen of the Netherlands, 99
Juvenile Bench, 111–12

Kaldor, Clarissa (now Lady), 137
Kaldor, Nicholas (later Baron), 47
Kennard, Amanda (granddaughter), 136
Kennard, David, 121
Kennard, Juliet (granddaughter), 136

Labour Party, 50, 51, 77–8, 137; signs of division, 83, 131; departure from, 131–2; GLC, 94, 104; LCC, 52, 94; Leeds, 47; Oxford University, 43, 44; Paddington, 49
Lambeth West District Health Authority, 135
Laski, Harold, 22
Lawrence, D. H., 30, 42
Layton, Sir Walter, 47
Layton, Lady, 28
Le Carré, John, 119
League of Nations, 46, 63
League of Nations Union, 3, 12, 15–16, 43–4, 50, 51, 63–4
Lee, Jenny (later Baroness), 47–8, 83
Lehmann, Rosamond, 21, 119
Lennard, Miss (babysitter), 68, 74
Leopold, Prince, 5

Index

Liddell, Alice, 5
Lizzie (nanny), 27, 66, 72, 75
Lloyd George, David, 74
London: Islington, 49, 56; Newington Lodge, 91–2, 96; Paddington, 46, 49, 50;. Toynbee Hall, 8; Wandsworth, 104. *See also* Hampstead
London County Council, 56–9, 83, 107–8, 131; Central Hackney, 56–7, 58, 68, 83; Children's Committee, 88, 107, 108; Labour Party, 52, 94; Education Committee, 57, 94, 107; North Battersea, 86; School Care Committee, 49–50, 56; Schools Committee, 88; Welfare Committee, 91–2
Longford, Frank Pakenham, Lord, 41
Lutyens, Sir Edwin, 127
Lympstone, 65
Lynd, Maire, 21, 31, 36, 137
Lynd, Robert, 21
Lynd, Sighle, 21

MacGillivray, Dr Barron, 122
McIntosh, Marjorie, 107–8
Macleod, Iain, 88
Macmillan, Harold (later Lord Stockton), 64
Macmillan, Maurice, 104
Malleson, Dr Joan, 73
Malvern Girls' College, 5, 17–19
Manchester, 1–4, 7, 11, 12; College of Technology, 6, 11
Margaret, Princess, 99, 128
Maternity Alliance, 85
Maxwell, Robert, 129
MENCAP, 125
Mentally Handicapped, Training of Staff for, Committee of Enquiry into, 123–4
Milan, 46
Mittler, Professor Peter, 125
Moncrieff, Sir Alan, 59
Morrison, Herbert (later Baron), 49, 52; as LCC leader, 56, 57, 58; as Home Secretary, 78, 84
Mount, Robin, 69
Murray, Freydis, 79
Murray, Professor Gilbert, 12

Nathan, Lady, 107
National Association for the Welfare of Children in Hospital, 60, 81
National Council of Voluntary Organizations, 129
National Development Group, 125
National Health Service, 85, 121–5, 128, 135
National Temperance Hospital, 81
New Statesman, 91
New York, 97, 129
Newsome, Noel, 69
Nicholas, Betty, 123
Nightingale, Florence, 59
Noble Combat, A (Duff and Von Trott), 41
Noel-Baker, Philip, 64, 90–91
North Camden Community Health Council, 110, 121–2
North London Collegiate School, 40, 89
North West Metropolitan Regional Hospital Board, 108, 109–11
Nursing Mirror, 124

Ogilvie, Lady (Mary Helen), 73
'One O'clock Clubs', 96
Owen, Dr David, 127, 132
Oxford, 4, 55, 59, 65–6; Dragon School, 41, 79; Park Town, 68, 79; Wykeham House, 5, 65
Oxford University, 34–44; All Souls, 29, 31, 35, 36, 40, 48, 70, 90; Labour Party, 43, 44; New College, 27, 36, 90, 112; Somerville College, 34, 35, 39–42, 132; Union, 41, 43–4, 90

Pakenham (later Mount), Julia, 40, 69
Palmer, Alfred (great-uncle), 24
Palmer, George (great-grandfather), 4–5
Palmer, George William (great-uncle), 5
Paris, 33
Parole Board, 108, 111, 132

Index

Parting of Ways, The (Duff), 37, 41
Patrick, Miss (St Paul's Girls' School), 20
Peace Ballot, 64
Pears, Sir Peter, 129
Piercey, Dr Jack, 91
Piercey, William, Baron, 48
Ploegstreet, 8
Plowden, Bridget (now Lady), 57, 79
Plowden, Edwin (now Baron), 57, 67, 79
Plowright, Dr Oliver, 54
Plowright, Pat, 129, 131
Population, Royal Commission on, 72–3, 84–5, 86
Population of Great Britain, The (Hubback), 72
Portofino, 46
Postbridge, 77, 105
Poulton, Edward (grandfather), 6, 22, 23–4, 54; Oxford home, 5, 42, 65
Poulton (*née* Palmer), Emily (grandmother), 4, 5, 23–4, 65; Oxford home, 5, 42; advice from, 18, 34
Poulton, Dr Edward P. (uncle), 7, 24
Poulton, Edward (cousin), 24
Poulton, Hilda (aunt), 9–10, 25
Poulton, Lily (aunt), 18
Poulton, Ronald (uncle), 6–8, 25, 100
Priestley, J. B., 13

Raikes, Simon, 138
Rea, Edward (grandson), 136
Rea, Emily, 136
Rea, Helen – *see* Jay, Helen
Rea, Rory, 136
Rea, Rupert Pennant (son-in-law), 136
Reading, 5, 7
Rees, Goronwy, 36–7, 42, 79
Reeves, Amber, 22
Remarque, Erich, 43
Ricks, Dr Derek, 123
Robinson, Kenneth, 108, 109
Rodgers, Barney, 131
Rodgers, Bill, 132
Rodgers, Margaret, 131
Rowse, A. L., 41
Royal College of Nursing, 124
Royal Free Hospital, 122
Ruskin, John, 5

St Paul's Girls' School, 19–22, 132, 137
Scholar Gypsy, The (Arnold), 19
Scott-James, Anne, 20
Serota, Bea (now Baroness), 107, 108, 110, 131
Sherriff, R. C., 43
Simon, Ernest (later Lord Simon of Wythenshawe), 11, 72, 84
Simon, Shena (later Lady), 11
Smiley's People (Le Carré), 119
Smuts, Jan Christian, 28
Snowdon, Lord, 99
Social Democratic Party, 132
Sofer, Anne, 132
Sokolov, Michael, 69
Somme, Battle of (1917), 9
Sons and Lovers (Lawrence), 42
Spastics Society, 125, 136
Spectator, 60
Spencer, Gilbert, 46, 51
Stauffenberg, Count Claus von, 41
Stocks, Mary, Baroness, 11
Sullivan, Ann, 131
Sullivan, David, 129, 131, 137
Summer Flood, The (Rees), 37
Supply, Ministry of, 67, 71
Sussex, University of, 98, 107
Symonds, Sir Charles (uncle), 10
Symonds, Lady (Janet Poulton), aunt, 25
Symonds, Richard (cousin), 10
Symonds, Ronald (cousin), 10

Temple, Archbishop of Canterbury, 7, 14
Testament of Youth (Britain), 43
Thatcher, Margaret, 111, 128, 129
Thomas, Derek, 123
Thomas, Mary (now Lady Jay), 102, 137, 138; first contact with, 95; deepening relationship with Douglas, 105–6, 114, 115; marriage, 121
Times, The, 29, 30, 35, 39, 46, 64, 113

Tokyo, 102
Trade, Board of, 94–5, 98
Trott, Adam von, 41

Van der Post, Ingrid, 106, 116, 120

Wade, Christopher, 129, 131
Wade, Diana, 129, 131
Waller (*née* Palmer), Alice, 5
Waller, Augustus, 5
Washington D.C., 113, 127–9
Watt, Miss (St Paul's Girls' School), 20
Webb, Sidney, 94
Week in Politics (TV programme), 129
Wells, H. G., 22
White, Anna Jane, 21–2
White, Justin Blanco, 21
Wigg, Miss (St Paul's Girls' School), 19
Wight, Isle of, 17, 68, 100, 120, 135; family holidays, 1, 3, 11–12, 23–6, 27–8, 38, 73–5, 89, 99, 117–18; parents' retirement to, 90; Horestone Cottage, 24–5, 49, 82, 117; Horestone Point, 11, 23, 25, 118; St Helen's Cottage, 23, 24, 28; Seagrove Bay, 1, 12, 25
Williams, Sir John Fischer, 40
Williams (later Hubback), Judy Fischer, 40
Williams, Prue Fischer, 40
Williams, Shirley, 132
Wilson, Harold (now Lord), 70, 79, 83, 94, 105
Wilson, Mary (now Lady), 70, 79
Wilson, Patsy, 129, 131
Winchester College, 89, 90
Window, The (Clayre), 121
Witt, John, 48
Witt, Margaret, 48
Wolf, Brit, 131
Wolf, Ed, 131
Wolfenden Report, 99
Woods, Miss (nanny), 17
Woods, Liz, 123–4
Woolf, Leonard, 51
Workers' Educational Association, 7
Wraxall Manor, 136
Wuthering Heights (Brontë), 75

Zell-am-See, 46